Illegitimi non curvu tyrannum

THE TYRANNY

OF WOKE

Death of the Social Contract

Phillip W. Smith

RSA Fellow of The Royal Society of Arts

Member of The Royal Society of Literature

ABOUT THE AUTHOR

Phillip Smith, that's me, was born in Canberra, Australia. After a career as a freelance musician and teacher, I moved to Norway to continue my life as a Strategic IT Consultant.

I have studied Music, IT, Education and Theology and hold a Master's Degree in Business Administration plus a career full of certificates, diplomas, self-help and technical courses and other collectibles.

I am a parent, a husband, a father and a male who identifies as male; my pronouns are the same as those used throughout the history of the English language and I believe that they do a perfectly adequate job. I am also white (but please don't tell anyone). I am in my 60's but "self-identify" as 50. So please don't age shame me?

ABOUT THIS BOOK

The *Tyranny of Woke* shines a light on the archetypal social contract that originated with Rousseau in 1762 to formalise the effective roles and responsibilities of both the sovereign and the people (see Appendix I). Today, most democracies have changed the role of the Sovereign from a King/Queen/Head-of-State and have elected, instead, a parliamentary body that is *supposedly* sovereign to the people; and within a wide-ranging mandate, based broadly, at least in intent, upon the issues that face our modern Society. The first three decades of the 21st century have already highlighted the division and tribalism that seems to be working its way into our "New Normal". From Churches and Religions to Universities and Schools, many of the prevailing assumptions of our society are being challenged in a way that has not occurred prior to our current internet age. This book examines, questions, criticises and reviews many of these new norms. I have not written it seeking your agreement nor do I wish in any way to offend. I was born in the 1950's and grew up in a world with real FREE speech and the ability to debate and discuss without having to worry about mis-gendering, micro aggressions, virtue signalling, critical race theory or whether the colour of one's skin makes you more or less entitled to life. We were able to do this because we believed in the right of people to hold contrary views to our own without trying to have them de-platformed, or stripped of their livelihood. As a humanist, I believe that all lives matter and are equally important and that Critical Race Theory[1] is evil, divisive, and fundamentally racist, and should never be allowed to dominate modern cultural discourse.

With very special thanks to me wife Sara, who put up with me day after day shouting; *"You have to see this baby. Its utterly unbelievable and ridiculous. This world is truly f***ed!"*

I am forever grateful for her support and companionship. She not only continually shows strength, courage and patience beyond the understanding of a mere male, but she also created the cover photographs for this book and my previous title; "A Benign Hypocrisy: The Separation of Church and Faith" (Smith) *Available in both Kindle and Paperback editions.*

---

[1] CRT is an intellectual movement and loosely organized framework of legal analysis based on the premise that race is not a natural, biologically grounded feature of physically distinct subgroups of human beings but a socially constructed (culturally invented) category that is being used to oppress and exploit people of colour.

"The "Woke" Tyranny" seeks to both entertain and challenge the reader to be open to criticism of some common held views and doctrines and encourage you, the reader, to think, explore, research and in the end, formulate your own well thought out conclusions and dogmas. I have loved writing it, in a strange way, and hope that you can both enjoy this book and find it challenging.

"Take the risk of thinking for yourself. Much more happiness, truth and beauty will come to you that way."
Christopher Hitchens

ABOUT THE APPENDICES

This work contains 3 appendices. The first is a public domain translation of the first 2 books of Rousseau's amazing work from 1762;

"The Social Contract"
Excerpt from
The Social Contract Jean-Jacques Rousseau
OR PRINCIPLES OF POLITICAL RIGHT 1762
Translated by G. D. H. Cole, public domain
Foederis æquas Dicamus leges. Virgil, Æneid xi.

I have included the first 2 books as they are the most relevant to this work and introduce the reader to the concept of the Social Contract as Rousseau defines it. The complete work consists of 6 books and was simply too long to include here. I strongly recommend that if you are curious about the birth and definition of the Social Contract and its relationship to Sovereignty and the people, then you will find it riveting reading with a rather excellent analysis by the translator.

Appendix II contains internet links to Two Treatises of Government by John Locke. This is another enlightenment age book of how to structure various forms of Government and society. An astonishing book with quite astonishing insight into the thinking during this tumultuous period of our history. Again, at 250 pages there seemed little point to include it here, but I think that anyone who finds the history of society and governments interesting, it is a most worthwhile addition. Again, the links are to the complete work and it is in downloadable PDF.

Appendix III is simply the complete poem from W.H.Audun, Funeral Blues. A deeply beautiful poem that gained fame and notoriety after its inclusion in the 1994 film, 4 Weddings and a Funeral.

In the film, the actor John Hannah is elegising his departed lover. It's a very moving and deeply beautiful moment of the movie and well worth the price of admission.

For someone like the speaker who has suffered a loss, the world is transformed. But to everyone else, nothing changes. Time doesn't slow down and no one cares what's happening. The indifference of the world plagues the speaker in this poem. They plead with the world to feel as they do, understand his grief, and even participate in it.

In a formal sense, "Funeral Blues" is a classic elegy. While the narrator does not go into specific detail about the loss suffered, the feelings of loss are very present. The text is referenced often in film and TV (such as in Four Weddings and a Funeral (ibid) and Gavin and Stacey). Auden structured the poem in four, four-line stanzas known as quatrains. These quatrains follow an AABB rhyming pattern, changing end sounds as the poet saw fit. It is an a typically sombre poem and is, therefore, a popular reading at funerals. Most of the poem is delivered through an omniscient, anonymous narrator. But as the lines go on, the amorphous loss becomes more personal the speaker makes use of first-person pronouns. The normal ones that we have used literally for centuries.

It is a beautiful poem and worth including in the appendices of this work.

WITH SINCERE THANKS

I would like to thank the authors of several specific books that I have read, used and or even quoted from in the writing of; The Tyranny of "Woke".

"Woke": A Guide to Social Justice.

>McGrath, Titania (Constable 2019)

"Free Speech and Why it Matters"

>Doyle, Andrew (Constable, 2021)

"The Madness of Crowds"

>Murray, Douglas (Bloomsbury Continuum, 2019 / 2021)

"The Third Wave: Micro-globalism and the coming employment crisis in Australia"

>Lindon Jones, Scott (2013)

"12 Rules for Life"

>Peterson, Jordan B (Random House, 2018)

"Beyond Order"

>Peterson, Jordan B (Portfolio, 2021)

"The Death of Right and Wrong"

Bruce, Tammy (Prima Lifestyles, 2003)

"On War"

Carl von Clausewitz (1874 1st ed. 1909 London, reprint)

"Innumeracy: Mathematical Illiteracy and Its Consequences"

Paulos, John Allen (Hill and Wang, 1989)

"Irreversible Damage: The Transgender Craze Seducing Our Daughters"

Shrier, Abigail (Regnery 2020)

"White Fragility: Why It's So Hard for White People to Talk About Racism"

Diangelo, Robin (Beacon Press, 2018) (pws: this one is utter garbage)

"The Authoritarian Moment: How the Left Weaponized America's Institutions Against Dissent"

Shapiro, Ben (Broadside Books 2021) (pws: utterly brilliant)

"How to Destroy America in Three Easy Steps"

Shapiro, Ben (Broadside Books 2020)

This list is not in any way exhaustive but it allows me to pay tribute to some of the truly brave and literate writers that have gone before me. In the fractured world in which we find ourselves, writing about topics such as "Woke", CRT, Gender, Education, Child Welfare, Cultural Appropriation, Virtue Signalling, White Fragility, Male Toxicity and Free Speech amongst others, can be fraught with dangerous outcomes. I hope that this book will honour those who have gone before and add my own unique voice to the most important social conversation that we have ever held. Not only for the sake of our future, but also for the conservancy of intelligent conversation over such vital and important issues that affect all of us and are today being shouted down by a very vocal minority.

Before we start, I really need to say a few short words about the amazing Titania McGrath[2]. She is in fact the alter ego creation of Andrew Doyle. Comedian, playwright, journalist, and political satirist from Northern Ireland, who co-wrote the fictional character Jonathan Pie and created the character Titania McGrath. He created Titania for a live comedy show which I truly wish I had seen. You can experience the same voice and style by purchasing "her" book as an audio book from Audible. It is all at once; biting in its satire, hysterically funny, beautifully acted (full credit to Alice Marshall) and written and simply one of my favourite books of the year. Some of Titania's most memorable quotes are used throughout this book at the beginning or end of some chapters. I hope you enjoy them in the spirit that they are intended. For example;

I had been breastfed for the first six months of my life. Did my mother not realise that I was a vegan? Did she even care? Either way, this was abuse. (McGrath)

And:

When queer activists appropriated the word 'gay' from its traditional meaning of 'happy', they achieved their goal of simultaneously increasing gayness and decreasing happiness. Such is the power of language. (McGrath)
(McGrath)

---

[2] Titania McGrath (@TitaniaMcGrath) is a parody Twitter account created and run by comedian and Spiked columnist Andrew Doyle. Doyle describes her as "a militant vegan who thinks she is a better poet than William Shakespeare".

If you think that you are already "Woke", then you really need to read or listen to "Woke": A Guide to Social Justice. *"Until you hear Titania, you just don't understand "woke"."*

PWS

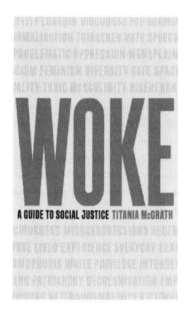

TABLE OF CONTENTS

About the author   2

About this book   2

   About the Appendices   4

With Sincere Thanks   6

Forward 14

   "Build-Back-Better"…what does it mean?   22

Part 1: Stay Woke... 26

The Divided States of America 26

   Origin of the Term   27

   We Killed it   29

   Rousseau and Locke   32

   Sacrificing Life, Liberty and Property   33

   Impact on the Founding Fathers   35

   A Social Contract for Everyone   36

   Popular Sovereignty   37

   Hobbes: Human Life in a State of Nature   38

   Locke: The Social Contract Limiting Ruler's Powers   38

   Rousseau: Who Makes the Laws?   39

   Popular Sovereignty and the US Government   40

   40 Years of Inadequate Moderates   42

Tyranny In The USA 45

   Plato on Tyranny   46

The Transgender Tsunami 54

   What is gender dysphoria?   56

   Monty Python: Life of Brian   71

Origins of "woke" **74**

"Woke" in the UK   **74**

Origin of the word "woke"   75

The twisting of "woke"   77

How is the word used now?   78

Is there another word to replace "woke"?   79

Part 2: Pure "Woke" Insanity **81**

Classical Music as Implicit White Supremacy   **81**

As Insufficiently Diverse   84

Constructing Beethoven as Black   90

The East Asian Affinity for Western classical music   92

Appreciation of Classical Music Correlated with Intelligence   94

Conclusion   97

Classical Music: An Alternate Truth   100

References: 106

Critical Race Theory: for Dummies **107**

What is it?   109

How it Works   111

Resistance is Futile   113

Political Engagement   115

Defeating the "Woke" Agenda   117

Talking About Race in the USA   119

Aspects and Assumptions of Whiteness and White Culture in the United States   120

Part 3: Wokeism, The Religion: Dogma of Hate **124**

"Woke" Word Salad **132**

White Fragility, Toxic Masculinity, The CISHET Dilemma, Male Fragility, Intersectionality and other Myths. 132

White Fragility 133

Toxic Masculinity 141

The "Cishet" Dilemma 142

Intersectionality 147

The Woke Prophet.................................... **148**

The Modern Left and Fascism 154

The Death of the Social Contract **159**

Politics no longer serves any 166

practical purpose 166

What social contract? 167

White People Should Stop Using The Term 'Woke' **169**

Part 4: Ouroboros.............................. **178**

Honestly 180

Maud Maron 182

The Perfervid Left 187

A New Enlightenment **190**

The End **200**

Appendices.................................... **201**

I: Rousseau 1762 .... **201**

The Social Contract **201**

Glossary 201

Book 1 **204**

1. The subject of the first book 205

2. The first societies 206

3.	The right of the strongest	209
4.	Slavery	210
5.	We must always go back to a first agreement	216
6.	The social compact	217
7.	The sovereign	220
8.	The civil state	224
9.	Real estate	225
Part 1 of Book 2		**229**
1.	Sovereignty is inalienable	229
2.	Sovereignty is indivisible	231
Conclusion		233

II: Two Treatises of Government *235*

III: Funeral Blues *236*

FORWARD

We are definitely living in extraordinary times.

For the third time in this century, the world has been exposed to a dangerous viral pandemic that started in China. The WHO[3] delayed in declaring a pandemic because China didn't want them to announce it until they had done their preparations and locked the people of Wuhan down, away from global scrutiny. It should be noted that the CCP[4] is the largest contributor country to the WHO. The CCP wields so much power over the WHO that Taiwan is not even recognised as a member state or even as an entity by the WHO. It simply does not exist in their opinion...or rather I should say, in the opinion of the CCP.

Meanwhile, western countries embarked on the largest post war spending spree since the 1940's. It is estimated that the USA, the EU, the UK, Scandinavia, Canada and Australia have spent more than 125 trillion dollars, expanding global debt to more than 190 trillion dollars. This at a time when the global economy is worth around 65 trillion dollars in total. This is a level of debt that simply will never be repaid. The ramifications of this are as yet, utterly unknown; but I am guessing that it won't be fabulous.

Countries are already decreasing the amount they pay in international aide to suffering nations as many of them are in default to the UN. As

---

[3] World Health Organisation
[4] Chinese Communist Party

14

a result, many UN programmes, entities, funds and activities will not be going ahead with the expected levels of funding through 2021-2022 or in fact anytime into the foreseeable future. Other aid agencies all over the world are screaming for money to support victims of war, victims of poverty and disease, nations under oppressive regimes, refugees and millions suffering through drought and terrorist attacks and starving in Yemen, Lebanon, Egypt, Libya, Tunisia, Syria, Iraq, Iran, Morocco and nearly all the rest of Africa and South and Latin America.

However, in the land of the free (?), what can now only be called The Divided States of America, they are consumed by a new religion; complete with Popes, High Priests even Prophets and punishments and sanctions. "Woke" culture has become Wokeism. Its clergy includes members of the houses of congress in the Divided States, parliamentarians in the dis-United Kingdom, MEPs[5] in the EU and politicians in Australia and Canada; The Wokeists.

In its fundamental ideology, Wokeism is neither Left nor Right but is a direct offshoot from, and the purest form of, Marxism[6] in the world today. It is increasingly clear that many of its followers come from the far left and many of its critics from the far right. The vast majority of voters internationally come from the centre. Wokeism is destroying education and the future of our children and in deed our entire society as we know

---

[5] Members of the European Parliament
[6] Extreme left – Socialist and extreme right – Fascist; are two sides of the same extremist ideology. Stalin was a both a communist and a fascist, as was Lenin and Mao.

it and as it was envisaged through the Enlightenment[7]; The Age of Reason.

In schools and universities across most western nations, students are being taught that to be born black means that you are oppressed and to be born white, Asian or middle eastern means that you are the Oppressor due to your perceived White Privilege.

To be born male means that you suffer from *toxic masculinity*, to be gay or lesbian, while not a true identity to the Wokeists, correspond to genders, but to be Transgender is seen as a legitimate identity to assume, whether or not you have commenced transitioning to the different gender of your birth or whether you simply claim that your identify is determined to be something other than your birth gender.

If someone had told me when I was 13 and very interested in Music, that I was exhibiting traits of a female, and sent me off to a Paediatric gender assignment clinic, I would have been very pissed off. In fact if you had told me that in the 21st Century there would even be such a thing as a paediatric gender assignment clinic, I simply would have laughed at you. Indeed, that is exactly what we should be doing today. Much more on that later.

---

[7] The Age of Enlightenment (also known as the Age of Reason or simply the Enlightenment) was an intellectual and philosophical movement that dominated the world of ideas in Europe during the 17th and 18th centuries. The Enlightenment included a range of ideas centred on the pursuit of happiness, sovereignty of reason, and the evidence of the senses as the primary sources of knowledge and advanced ideals such as liberty, progress, toleration, fraternity, constitutional government, and separation of church and state.

I am neither left nor right. In my adopted country, I cannot vote except in local elections. So I happily tread the path of an independent thinker who leans towards the conservative centre. Particularly in the areas of Social Justice, Political Correctness and Wokeism.

I adhere strongly and philosophically to the original intent of the Social Contract between the People and the Sovereign. Particularly in Rousseau; *In a democracy, the whole people constitute a sovereign, and individual citizens are members of the sovereign.*

I believe that the current nonsense in regard to Wokeism and Wokeists, will surely pass away and common sense and the spirit of community will survive and return even stronger. To try to divide people on the basis of Race, Gender, Sexual Preference or anything else so arbitrary, is basically the antithesis of what modern Western societies have striven to achieve throughout the past 2 or 3 centuries. The very fact that the wokeists use terms such as, Transgenderphobia, Islamophobia, White privilege, Toxic Masculinity, Intersectionality etc. is anathema to an evolved modern society. There are more terms for the dogma of the new religion than there are observants to its doctrine of hatred and division. Do children as young as 3 and 4 years old really deserve to be taught that they are; innately oppressors of the black people who are and always will be oppressed; and that they need to shed all aspects of their whiteness? I think not!

This book really is for those who, like me, are sick and tired of being yelled at from the talking heads on Global Network Television, telling

17

me to atone for the sins of my distant relatives. My relatives actually came from Poland, England, France and Switzerland. It is self-evident that the records of my polish Jewish grandparents and their families, no longer actually exist, for obvious reasons. If I have white privilege, where does it come from? How did I catch it? Is there a vaccine for that?

I hope this book can help you to understand the rubbish that is being spread throughout the west in our life time, and arm you with some interesting and horrifying facts for that next terrifying dinner you attend when the "woke", black, lesbian, intersectional, transgender, Muslim, sits across the table from you and says; "Do you think Black Lives matter and that they should defund the police?"

The correct answers is of course; Well, yes and no. I believe that all lives matter and that defunding the police is quite possibly the most stupid and dangerous idea ever put forward as part of a political platform…but be prepared to run ☺…Wokeists are not forgiving. If you turn the other cheek, they'll just smack you on that one as well.

I have included the next section about Build-Back-Better as a guide to what that expression means and where it originated. Like all the "woke" terminology, Build-Back-Better is another perfervid statement. It grew out of the World Economic Forum, held each year at Davos in Switzerland; a hugely expensive ski resort where several hundred of the worlds, super rich, movers and shakers, gather to determine the best way for the plebs to live their miserable lives.

The expression started its etymological journey as "The Great Reset"[8]. Another piece of Marxist ideology, concerned with the removal of the concept of private ownership of anything, unless of course you're rich enough to attend Davos, single world government, global health care and global taxation.

I can only assume that at some point during the past few years, it was felt that; *"The Great Reset" is just too triggering for the earths 7.8 billion inhabitants, so let's use a code that only us elites will understand. I know...how about "Build-Back-Better"?*

What on earth does that even mean?

Exactly, the public won't even know what we mean by it, but if, slowly, we all start using it, it will be just like the Covid lockdowns. They'll just end up nodding along without even realising that we are preparing for "The Great Reset".

Conspiracy Theory? Maybe. But in case it's not and this is, in fact, underway, pay attention to how many politicians and Davos goers start using, Build-Back-Better as part of their political posturing of societal elements such as taxation, health care, housing, student debt, Universal Basic Income etc. Now, when you also consider that the scary Klaus Schwab[9] is not only current Executive Chairman, but he was also the

---

[8] https://www.weforum.org/great-reset
[9] The World Economic Forum is chaired by Founder and Executive Chairman Professor Klaus Schwab. https://en.wikipedia.org/wiki/Klaus_Schwab

founder. He founded this club-med style economic extravaganza for the uber rich while in his 30s and today is still chairman. So no fresh, young blood going on here. But hey, if you still think there is nothing to see here, then look at some of Herr Schwab's economic ideas and videos. If you are not horrified and shocked, then just google The World Economic Forum and find out who goes to Davos. The world's best economists? No. Elected officials from every country? No, but plenty of rich white guys. The guest list includes the Crown Prince of Norway and wife, The Unelected heads of the EU, Bill Gates, Harvey Weinstein, Geoffrey Epstein, Elon Musk, Prince Harry and Meghan, Oprah Winfrey, Obama and of course, the Clintons. It is a celebrity and uber rich snow festival over 4 glorious days.

During Davos each year, the small local airfield hosts more private planes than any other airfield on earth. During the celebrity fuelled "conference" earlier last year, the small local airfield published this photo of just some of the planes that had arrived early on the first day. By the end of that day, the local airfield had to ask pilots and owners of the other jets to please move their aircraft to a regional airport so that the uber wealthy could park close to the resort. I kid you not.

And all this in 2020, the year that Klaus decided that the WEF this year would focus on Climate Change…lol. If this wasn't so corrupt and obscene, it would be hysterically funny.

Private jets line up at World Economic Forum as they focus on Climate change.

"BUILD-BACK-BETTER"...WHAT DOES IT MEAN?

On October 14, 2020, Mark Tovey[10] published the following article with the MISES Institute.[11]

The Trump campaign shared a video on social media this week, claiming Joe Biden had ripped off a slogan from British prime minister Boris Johnson.

"We have a great opportunity to build back and to Build-Back-Better" (emphasis added), Biden said in the video, dated July 9, 2020. Then rolled a video of the British PM, using the same phrase on May 28: "We owe it to future generations to Build-Back-Better." Damning evidence, it seemed, that the Democratic nominee had, once again, copied his homework. (Biden was famously caught passing off a Robert F. Kennedy quote as his own during his ill-fated 1988 run for president.)

In fact, the story here is not one of lazy speech writing or plagiarism. The use of the phrase "Build-Back-Better" by both Biden and the British

---

[10] Mark Tovey works for a data news agency and has authored numerous reports for London-based think-tanks, including the Institute of Economic Affairs and the Taxpayers' Alliance. His research has largely focused on health economics issues and the UK foreign aid budget. He graduated in 2016 with a degree in economics from the University of Sussex.

[11] The Mises Institute, founded in 1982, teaches the scholarship of Austrian economics, freedom, and peace. The liberal intellectual tradition of Ludwig von Mises (1881-1973) and Murray N. Rothbard (1926-1995) guides them. Accordingly, the Mises Institute seeks a profound and radical shift in the intellectual climate: away from statism and toward a private property order. The Mises Institute encourages critical historical research, and stands against political correctness.

PM spells something far more sinister. "Build-Back-Better" is the rallying cry of a globalist plot to exploit the coronavirus pandemic for the sake of narrow-minded, well-connected lobby groups; particularly of the "environmentalist" stripe.

Boris Johnson did not coin the phrase "Build-Back-Better". It first surfaced on April 22 in a UN press release, marking "International Mother Earth Day"; a faux holiday created by the UN in 2009.

As the world begins planning for a post-pandemic recovery, the United Nations is calling on Governments to seize the opportunity to "Build-Back-Better" by creating more sustainable, resilient and inclusive societies.

"The current crisis is an unprecedented wake-up call," said Secretary-General António Guterres in his International Mother Earth Day message. "We need to turn the recovery into a real opportunity to do things right for the future."

But would "Brexit Boris" really swallow a globalist scheme, hook, line and sinker? On October 6, the British PM unveiled a plan at the Conservative Party conference to dump £160m into powering every home with wind energy by 2030—all part of a harebrained scheme to "build back greener."

The Conservative lawmaker Lord Matt Ridley excoriated Boris's "build back greener" policy in a radio interview the next day: "It takes 150 tonnes of coal to build one wind turbine...if we want a zero-carbon future by 2050, the only way we're going to get it is nuclear. Wind is messing around and rewarding rich people at the expense of poor people."

But it is not just Boris Johnson and Joe Biden who are being played like cheap violins by the UN. All around the world, politicians are echoing the same sentiment.

The European Commission used the slogan when announcing their €750 billion stimulus fund on May 27: "Through this fund, officially titled Next Generation EU, the Commission hopes to "Build-Back-Better," through channels that contribute to a greener, more sustainable and resilient society."

In Canada, PM Justin Trudeau signalled his allegiance to the globalist "green" lobby in August, saying: "We need to reset the approach of this government for a recovery to Build-Back-Better."

The UN have even taken the liberty of translating the slogan into *Spanish* (reconstruirmejor), *Portuguese* (reconstruirmelho),

French (reconstruire en mieux), and many other tongues—so that politicians all over the world can sing from the same hymn sheet. The No Agenda podcast, hosted by Adam Curry and John C. Dvorak, is a fantastic resource for keeping track of the growing number of co-occurrences of the "Build-Back-Better" meme.

Some environmentalists are twisting the covid-19 pandemic into a pretext for extreme "green" policies, of the type that would have been unthinkable less than a year ago. During lockdown, countless commentators waxed lyrical about how "nature was coming back to life" during our miserable home imprisonment. Now, economist Mariana Mazzucato, of University College London, is floating the idea of "climate lockdowns". That is, forcing people to stay in their homes to limit carbon dioxide emissions. The UN is pushing a global propaganda campaign to get a good percentage of national bailout budgets siphoned off into "green" gravy train projects with highly questionable environmental and economic returns.

Talk of "Build-Back-Better" and "green growth" obfuscates the trade-off between growing GDP and limiting carbon dioxide emissions. Globally, GDP is forecast to plummet a whopping 5.8 percent in 2021 according to the International Monetary Fund.

Lifting lockdowns, cutting taxes and deregulating would quickly get the world turning again. On the other hand, financing a global racket with billions of dollars of funny money or "Build-Back-Better" will only cause us to sink deeper into this malaise.

So strap in, secure your tray tables, stow all belongings under the seat in front of you; as we explore the inverted world of "Woke".

PART I:

STAY WOKE

THE DIVIDED STATES OF AMERICA

On the matter of the President of the United States (PotUS):
How do you get to be PotUS if you're a sociopath?
How do you get to be PotUS if you're not?

The term "Social Contract" refers to the idea that the state exists

only to serve the will of the people, who are the source of all political power enjoyed by the state. The people can choose to give or with-hold this power. The idea of the social contract is one of the founda-tions of the American / British / Australian / Canadian and most of the Wests, political systems.

Yet, today it would be correct to observe that the concept of any form of Social Contract is no longer a principal that supports a vi-brant society. The false belief that the United States is in any way democratic in 2021 has to be resigned to the faded memories of the past and into the fading brilliance of a more enlightened historical age.

ORIGIN OF THE TERM

The term "social contract" can be found as far back as the writings of the 4th-5th century BCE Greek philosopher Plato. However, it was English philosopher Thomas Hobbes (1588–1679) who ex-panded on the idea when he wrote "Leviathan," his philosophical response to the English Civil War. In the book, he wrote that in early human history there was no government. Instead, those who were the strongest could take control and use their power over others at any time. His famous summation of life in "NATURE" (before government) is that it was "solitary, poor, nasty, brutish, and short."

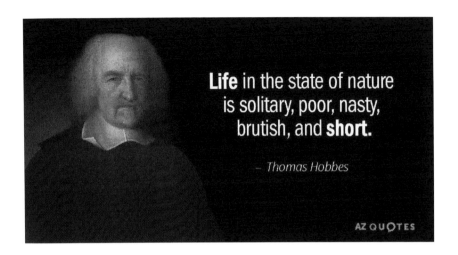

Life in the state of nature is solitary, poor, nasty, brutish, and **short.**

– Thomas Hobbes

AZ QUOTES

Hobbes' theory was that in the past, the people mutually agreed to create a state, giving it only enough power to provide protection of their well-being. However, in Hobbes' theory, once the power was given to the state, the people then relinquished any right to that power. In effect, the loss of rights was the price of the protection they sought. This is the alarming truth of the world's modern democracies. You need look no further than the United States and the European Union to observe just how many of our, fiercely fought for, liberties we have surrendered to undemocratic, bureaucracies and obscure political structures. The concept of government with very limited powers; with a mandate to serve the people of the nation; and that is accountable, in every regard, to the will of the people; would seem to be totally dead.

The Social Contract no longer exists between political bodies, parliaments, congresses or presidents and the people they serve. In fact, I would argue that the very premise of the Social Contract has been totally reversed; and it is us, The People, who now serve the political structures.

The Social Contract is not just dead. It has been slaughtered upon the altar of false democracy, out of control spending, illegal taxation and un-representative government. The professional politician is the new normal. Politicians have created a long term career path for themselves in what should have been a vibrant and democratically representative form of government. In the EU, The USA, most of Latin America, all of Africa and Australia and New Zealand, Politicians go from local government, to federal government, to the UN or one of its agencies, the EU or one of its 9 presidents, and then back to their home country often as an unelected advisor or even President; all without any regard for the "will of the people". They just appoint each other to continuous jobs for life.

We have totally surrendered our sovereignty for the myth of stable democracy. The EU parliament has no governing authority. It cannot propose, suggest, modify, edit or cancel any bills, laws, rules or regulations that govern the member states of the EU. All of that must come from the European Council. An unelected group of "leaders". So just what exactly do the over 35,000 employees of the EU do each day? The US has elections that are limited to one of two parties. The people that run for election are chosen by the parties. For example; how many US citizens actually voted for who they wanted as President? None.

The two useless parties selected two useless candidates, Trump and Biden. US citizens have no say in it at all. How many of them voted for

Kamala Harris to be Vice-President and the next president if anything happens to Joe (which, let's face it, is stunningly likely). None. Even when they are invited to vote, they actually only elect a certain number of electors depending on the population of the state. These un-named, un-elected folk who form the Electoral College, then go away for a junket in some city and cast their votes for who will be the next president. Are they bound to vote the way that the electors selected? No, actually. They can, if they so desire, vote in an opposite way than they have been instructed by the state they represent. So why ask the people what they want at all? American Elections are nothing more than theatre obscura.

Is it any wonder that an obscene and violent, Marxist ideology is now rampant over the globe. Revolution has always loved unrest. The trouble is that in the 21st Century, despite having plenty to be "un-restful" about, we have largely become societies of extreme tolerance to bad ideas and appalling decisions. We have surrendered the only thing that we should never give up; Our Sovereignty. Sadly, we have already surrendered our freedom(s).

People have died for centuries before now to retain and maintain the sovereignty of the people. We just turn up to un-democratic elections, vote for candidates we know nothing about who we know will lie and cheat just to get a government pay cheque. Will never be fired no matter how disgusting their behaviour and will serve in our bizarre parliamentary systems for as long as they like due to the complete lack of oversight from the people.

A Recipe for the Future

Start by rejecting immoral and illegal mandates from our politicians. Stop judges from freeing rapists and murderers while jailing tax dodgers and journalists. Demand democratic representation and abolish lifelong political terms. Every single public servant role in any administration should be limited to 4 years. Then make them serve at least 4 years in the private sector before returning to public service, should they wish and if they are elected. Public Bureaucracies are now the largest employer in any "democratic" society of the Western World. They too can not be fired unless they kill someone and even then it's probably difficult. How did we let this happen? Why do we tolerate the appalling service we get from tax payer funded agencies. Why are rude and unhelpful people, simply to be tolerated in our agencies and entities. It is our government and we should start by taking it back.

We had better do it soon or else we will find ourselves trying to survive in a Marxist state; and history shows us that that's not a good place to be…unless you're at the top of that society. No wonder so many politicians are embracing Marxist ideology and policies and no wonder we have lost our voice in our systems of governance.

"Stop all the clocks, cut off the telephone,
Prevent the dog from barking with a juicy bone,
Silence the pianos and with muffled drum
Bring out the coffin, let the mourners come."[12]
The Social Contract is dead!

---

[12] W.H.Auden "Funeral Blues" (see appendix III for the complete text of this extraordinary poem).

The Swiss philosopher Jean Jacques Rousseau (1712–1778) and English philosopher John Locke (1632–1704) each took the social contract theory one step further. In 1762, Rousseau wrote "The Social Contract, Or Principles of Political Right," in which he explained that government is based on the idea of popular sovereignty. The essence of this idea is that the will of the people as a whole gives power and direction to the state.

John Locke based many of his political writings on the idea of the social contract. He stressed the role of the individual and the idea that in a "state of nature," people are essentially free. When Locke referred to the "state of nature," he meant that people have a natural state of independence, and they should be free "to order their actions, and dispose of their possessions and persons, as they think fit, within the bounds of the law of nature." Locke argued that people are thus not royal subjects, but in order to secure their property rights, people willingly give over their right to a central authority to judge whether a person is going against the laws of nature and needed to be punished.

The type of government is less important to Locke (except for absolute despotism): Monarchy, aristocracy, and republic are all acceptable forms of government as long as that government provides and protects the basic rights of life, liberty, and property to the people. Locke further argued that if a government no longer protects each individual's right, then revolution is not just a right but an obligation.

SACRIFICING LIFE, LIBERTY AND PROPERTY

This is a very interesting element in Locke's work. How can we justify, under these "rights" things such as Covid Lockdowns, Mask Mandates, Social Distancing and Vaccine Passports. All of these do impede the rights of individuals to life, liberty and property. Don't get me wrong, I am not suggesting that Covid restrictions and rules are an acceptable excuse for revolution, although I'm sure Locke would have; Rather that under certain circumstances and in the interests of the wellbeing and welfare of the majority, it may be necessary to introduce temporary and important restrictions on one's personal freedoms. Given the lens of Covid, this seems perfectly logical and possibly even the right thing to do. I know that opinions vary, but the reality is that the world has largely agreed to forego certain rights and privileges in the interests, hope and belief, that this is necessary to protect the people. I only bring this up at all as you are, should you decide to read further, about to enter the world of "Woke" politics. You will see that the rights and privileges of a silent majority are being sacrificed at the altar of Wokeism at the behest of a very noisy minority. Civil rights and human rights, even parenting rights are being destroyed.

Over 400 years of civilization, learning, science and experience are being thrown away in the interests of minorities. Some have a legitimate claim to having suffered at the hands of white people during the era of slavery. Which ended, by the way, with the Emancipation Declaration (signed January 1st, 1863). I know, the civil war didn't end until 1865 but the proclamation declared "that all persons held as slaves" within the rebellious states "are, and henceforward shall be free." So let's take that date as a line in the sand. It is a matter of common knowledge that very few real improvements were made to the life conditions of African Americans until the victories of the civil rights movement during the 60's and 70's. Yes, the US has been unbelievably slow to adopt new social mores[13]...usually.

The transgender issue that is destroying universities, schools, families and the rights of woman globally. The country with the highest percentage of the population that identify as trans is, surprise surprise, the United States with 0.58% of the population who identify as trans. When I say that Wokeism is being driven by a loud minority...I am absolutely not making it up.

But I digress. More on these topics in a later section. Back to the Social Contract.

---

[13] Mores (pronounced: morays) are social norms that are widely observed within a particular society or culture. Mores determine what is considered morally acceptable or unacceptable within any given culture.

IMPACT ON THE FOUNDING FATHERS

The idea of the social contract had a huge impact on the American Founding Fathers[14], especially Thomas Jefferson[15] (1743–1826) and James Madison[16] (1751–1836). The US Constitution starts with the three words, "We the people...," embodying this idea of popular sovereignty in the very beginning of this key document.

Following from this principle, a government established by the free choice of its people is required to serve the people, who in the end have sovereignty, or supreme power, to keep or overthrow that government.

Jefferson and John Adams (1735–1826), often political rivals, agreed in principle but disagreed about whether a strong central government (Adams and the federalists) or a weak one (Jefferson

---

[14] The term "Founding Fathers" is often used to refer to the 56 signers of the Declaration of Independence in 1776. It should not be confused with the term "Framers." According to the National Archives, the Framers were the delegates to the 1787 Constitutional Convention who drafted the proposed Constitution of the United States.

[15] Thomas Jefferson (April 13, 1743–July 4, 1826) was the third president of the United States, after George Washington and John Adams. His presidency is perhaps best known for the Louisiana Purchase, a single land transaction that doubled the size of the United States' territory. Jefferson was an anti-Federalist who was wary of a large central government and favoured states' rights over federal authority.

[16] James Madison (March 16, 1751–June 28, 1836) served as America's 4th president, navigating the country through the War of 1812. Madison was known as the "Father of the Constitution," for his role in its creation, and a man who served during a key time in the development of America.
'

and the Democratic-Republicans) sufficed best for supporting the social contract.

A SOCIAL CONTRACT FOR EVERYONE

As with many philosophical ideas behind the political theory, the Social Contract has inspired various forms and interpretations and has been evoked by many different groups throughout American and Western history.

Revolutionary-era Americans favoured Social Contract theory over the British Tory concepts of patriarchal government and looked to the social contract as support for the rebellion. During the antebellum[17] and Civil War periods, social contract theory was used by all sides. Enslavers used it to support states' rights and succession, Whig party moderates upheld the social contract as a symbol of continuity in government, and abolitionists found support in Locke's theories of natural rights.

More recently, historians also have linked Social Contract theories to pivotal social movements such as those for Native American rights, civil rights, immigration reform, and women's rights. Are we now witnessing the death of the Social Contract?

---

[17] existing before a war especially: existing before the American Civil War

- *Dienstag, Joshua Foa. "Between History and Nature: Social Contract Theory in Locke and the Founders." The Journal of Politics 58.4 (1996): 985–1009.*
- *Hulliung, Mark. "The Social Contract in America: From the Revolution to the Present Age." Lawrence: University Press of Kansas, 2007.*
- *Lewis, H.D. "Plato and the Social Contract." Mind 48.189 (1939): 78–81.*
- *Riley, Patrick. "Social Contract Theory and its Critics." Goldie, Mark and Robert Worker (eds.), The Cambridge History of Eighteenth-Century Political Thought, Volume 1. Cambridge: Cambridge University Press, 2006. 347–375.*
- *White, Stuart. "Review Article: Social Rights and Social Contract—Political Theory and the New Welfare Politics." British Journal of Political Science 30.3 (2000): 507–32.*

POPULAR SOVEREIGNTY

The *popular sovereignty* principle is one of the underlying ideas of the United States Constitution, and it argues that the source of governmental power (sovereignty) lies with the people (popular). This tenet is based on the concept of the Social Contract[18], the idea that government should be for the benefit of its citizens. If the government is not protecting the people, says the Declaration of Independence, it should be dissolved. That idea evolved through the writings of Enlightenment philosophers from England; Thomas Hobbes (1588–1679) and John Locke

---

[18] Refer Chapter 1, <u>The Social Contract in American Politics</u>

(1632–1704); and from Switzerland, Jean Jacques Rousseau (1712–1778).

HOBBES: HUMAN LIFE IN A STATE OF NATURE

Thomas Hobbes wrote *The Leviathan* in 1651, during the English Civil War, and in it, he laid out the first basis of popular sovereignty. According to his theory, human beings were selfish and if left alone, in what he called a "state of nature," human life would be "nasty, brutish, and short." Therefore, to survive people give over their rights to a ruler who provides them with protection. In Hobbes' opinion, an absolute monarchy provided the best form of security.

LOCKE: THE SOCIAL CONTRACT LIMITING RULER'S POWERS

John Locke wrote *Two Treatises on Government*[19] in 1689, in response to another paper (Robert Filmer's *Patriarcha*) which argued that kings have a "divine right" to rule. Locke said that the power of a king or government doesn't come from God, but comes from the people. People make a "social contract" with their government, trading away some of their rights to the ruler in exchange for security and laws.

---

[19] https://bit.ly/john_locke

In addition, Locke said, individuals have natural rights including the right to hold property. The government does not have the right to take this away without their consent. Significantly, if a king or ruler breaks the terms of the "contract"—by taking away rights or taking away property without an individual's consent—it is the right of the people to offer resistance and, if necessary, depose him.

ROUSSEAU: WHO MAKES THE LAWS?

Jean Jacques Rousseau wrote *The Social Contract*[20] in 1762. In this, he proposes that "Man is born free, but everywhere he is in chains." These chains are not natural, says Rousseau, but they come about through the "right of the strongest," the unequal nature of power and control.

According to Rousseau, people must willingly give legitimate authority to the government through a "social contract" for mutual preservation. The collective group of citizens who have come together must make the laws, while their chosen government ensures their daily implementation. In this way, the people as a sovereign group look out for the common welfare as opposed to the selfish needs of each individual.

---

[20] Man is born free, and everywhere he is in chains. Here's one who thinks he is the master of others, yet he is more enslaved than they are. How did this change come about? I don't know. What can make it legitimate?

POPULAR SOVEREIGNTY AND THE US GOVERNMENT

The idea of popular sovereignty was still evolving when the founding fathers were writing the US Constitution during the Constitutional Convention of 1787. In fact, popular sovereignty is one of six foundational principles on which the convention built the US Constitution. The other five principles are a limited government, the separation of powers, a system of checks and balances, the need for judicial review, and federalism, the need for a strong central government. Each tenet gives the Constitution a basis for authority and legitimacy that it uses even today.

Popular sovereignty was often cited before the US Civil War as a reason why individuals in a newly organized territory should have the right to decide whether or not the practice of enslavement should be allowed. The Kansas-Nebraska Act of 1854 was based on the idea—that people have a right to "property" in the form of enslaved people. It set the stage for a situation that became known as Bleeding Kansas[21], and it is a painful irony because certainly Locke and Rousseau would not agree that people are ever considered property.

---

[21] Bleeding Kansas refers to the time between 1854 and 1859 when the Kansas territory was the site of much violence over whether the territory would be free or allow enslavement.

As Rousseau wrote in "The Social Contract":

"From whatever aspect we regard the question, the right of slavery is null and void, not only as being illegitimate, but also because it is absurd and meaningless. The words slave and right contradict each other, and are mutually exclusive." (Rousseau)

Sources and further reading

- *Deneys-Tunney, Anne. "Rousseau shows us that there is a way to break the chains—from within." The Guardian, July 15, 2012.*
- *Douglass, Robin. "Fugitive Rousseau: Slavery, Primitivism, and Political Freedom." Contemporary Political Theory 14.2 (2015): e220–e23.*
- *Habermas, Jurgen. "Popular sovereignty as procedure." Eds., Bohman, James, and William Rehg. Deliberative Democracy: Essays on Reason and Politics. Cambridge, MA: MIT Press, 1997. 35–66.*
- *Hobbes, Thomas. "The Leviathan, or the Matter, Forme, & Power of a Common-Wealth Ecclesiasticall and Civill." London: Andrew Crooke, 1651. McMaster University Archive of the History of Economic Thought. Hamilton, ON: McMaster University.*
- *Locke, John. "Two Treastises of Government." London: Thomas Tegg, 1823. McMaster University Archive of the History of Economic Thought. Hamilton, ON: McMaster University.*
- *Morgan, Edmund S. "Inventing the People: The Rise of Popular Sovereignty in England and America." New York, W.W. Norton, 1988.*
- *Reisman, W. Michael. "Sovereignty and Human Rights in Contemporary International Law." American Journal of International Law 84.4 (1990): 866–76. Print.*
- *Rousseau, Jean-Jacques. The Social Contract. Trans. Bennett, Jonathan. Early Modern Texts, 2017.*

Citation: Kelly, Martin. "Popular Sovereignty." ThoughtCo, Feb. 16, 2021, thoughtco.com/popular-sovereignty-105422.

INSANITY

Voting for the same destructive parties over and over, expecting different results.

40 YEARS OF INADEQUATE MODERATES

Ronald Reagan: showed us that even an actor could become president.

Bush snr: showed us that it is ok for the president to invade a country to benefit his family's Oil Company.

Bill Clinton: showed us that to be president you didn't need to have any morals at all.

Bush jr: Showed that an intellect was optional to be president, as long as you went back and finished the war that dad started.

Barak Obama: proved that keeping electoral promises is completely optional for the president, just as long as you keep starting more and more wars in foreign countries…and drone your enemies and even US citizens with complete impunity.

Donald Trump: Demonstrated that the US didn't actually need a president but that literally anyone could get the job.

Joe Biden: is showing us that you don't even need to show up to be president.

Not exactly a long list of stellar intellects here I'm afraid. So, what does the last 40 years of US presidents tell us about the country?

I think it demonstrates clearly that anyone with even half an aware brain cell, obviously doesn't vote! In the 2020 US election, both candidates received more votes than any other candidate in American History. The Fact that Joe Biden, apparently, received more than 75 million votes is nothing short of astonishing…but not in a good way. He is a senior citizen who is so obviously suffering from dementia and possibly alzheimer's. This is in every sense of the word, Elder Abuse. I don't know what his family and friends are thinking but he really should be home in his basement watching TV not making a string of erratic and very poorly executed decisions and policies that will see the US carrying the largest debt of any nation…ever! That is terrible for the country, horrible for the citizens and their children, and potentially disastrous for the world economy. It will, in fact, almost perfectly play into the hands of China as they leverage the US debt to take the world away from the US dollar being the unit of the global Reserve Currency and shifting it to China. I am no economist but if that were to happen, and I can't see any way that it won't, the impact on global trade and economies can only be imagined. But I am fairly sure it won't be wonderful, certainly not for the US.

I think what I would now call the "Woke" supremacy, now spreading ridiculously rapidly across the world, will ultimately destroy itself. Like all Marxist based governments, they cannot survive the test of time and will devour themselves eventually. The question for those of us who oppose it is; at what cost? Will we;

- defund the police and enter a phase of crime driven anarchy,
- destroy the education standards that we have built over centuries,
- abuse and confuse a whole generation of young children with our insane views of 75 -100 or more different genders and the evil medical intervention of the Paediatric Gender Reassignment Clinics (this one sounds like something out of the Nazi playbook and Dr Mengele)

Or, will sanity and maturity prevail and the common sense of a meritocracy and the clear relevance of the Social Contract, be restored? Hope for an end to stupidity, an end to anarchy, an end to child abuse, and an end to constantly voting into our parliaments; geriatrics, idiots, racists, bigots and liars.

We can only hope.

"A house divided against itself cannot stand"
Abraham Lincoln

TYRANNY[22] IN THE USA

The ideal subject of totalitarian rule is not the convinced Nazi or the dedicated communist, but people for whom the distinction between fact and fiction (i.e., the reality of experience) true and false (i.e., the standards of thought) no longer exists.

HANNAH ARENDT, The Origins of Totalitarianism[23]

[As] he listened to the cries of joy rising from the town, Rieux remembered that such joy is always imperilled. He knew what those jubilant crowds did not know but could have learned from books: that the plague bacillus never dies or disappears for good; that it can lie dormant for years and years in furniture and linen chests; that it bides its time in bedrooms, cellars, trunks, and bookshelves; and that perhaps the day would come when, for the bane and the enlightening of men, it would rouse up its rats again and send them forth to die in a happy city.

ALBERT CAMUS, The Plague[24]

From: How Democracies Become Tyrannies
By Ed Kaitz

February 16, 2009

For those who want to be left alone to realize their capacities and talents this (USA) is an ideal country.
ERIC HOFFER[25] (1959).

"That was then. This is now. Flash forward fifty years to the election of Barack Obama and a hard left leaning Democrat Congress. What Americans want today, apparently, is a government that has no intention of leaving any of them alone. "

---

[22] Cruel, unreasonable, or arbitrary use of power or control.

[23] Hannah Arendt, The Origins of Totalitarianism (New York, Harcourt, Inc., 1976), 474.

[24] Albert Camus, The Plague, translated from the French by Stuart Gilbert (New York: Vintage Books, 1991), 308.

[25] Eric Hoffer was an American moral and social philosopher. He was the author of ten books and was awarded the Presidential Medal of Freedom in February 1983. Sadly he died later in May 1983. His first book, The True Believer, was widely recognized as a classic, receiving critical acclaim from both scholars and laymen, although Hoffer believed that The Ordeal of Change was his finest work. Wikipedia

"How could Hoffer have been so wrong about America? Why did America change so quickly? Can a free people willingly choose servitude? Is it possible for democracies to become tyrannies? And how is it possible in the 21st century."

PLATO ON TYRANNY

The answers to these questions were famously addressed in a few pages tucked within the greatest masterpiece of the classical world: Plato's *Republic*. On the surface, and to most reviewers of Plato's writings, the *Republic* is a dialogue on justice and on what constitutes the just society. But to careful readers the deeper theme of the *Republic* is the nature of education and the relationship between education and the survival of the state. In fact, the *Republic* is essentially the story of how a man (Socrates) condemned to death for "corrupting" the youth of Athens gives to posterity the most precious gift of all: the love of wisdom.

In the *Republic*, two young men, Glaucon and Adeimantus, accompany the much older Socrates on a journey of discovery into the nature of the individual soul and its connection to the harmony of the state. During the course of their adventure, as the two disciples demonstrate greater maturity and self-control, they are gradually exposed to deeper and more complex teachings regarding the relationship between virtue, self-sufficiency, and happiness. In short, the boys begin to realise that justice and happiness in a community rests upon the moral condition of its citizens. This is what Socrates meant when he said: "The state is man writ large."

Near the end of the *Republic,* Socrates decides to drive this point home by showing Adeimantus what happens to a regime when its parents and educators neglect the proper moral education of its children. In the course of this chilling illustration Adeimantus comes to discover a dark and ominous secret: without proper moral conditioning a regime's "defining principle" will be the source of its ultimate destruction. For democracy, that defining principle is freedom. According to Socrates, freedom *makes* a democracy but freedom also eventually *breaks* a democracy.

For Socrates, democracy's "insatiable desire for freedom and neglect of other things" end up putting it "in need of a dictatorship." The short version of his theory is that the combination of freedom and poor education in a democracy render the citizens incapable of mastering their impulses and deferring gratification. The reckless pursuit of freedom leads the citizens to raze moral barriers, deny traditional authority, and abandon established methods of education. Eventually, this uninhibited quest for personal freedom forces the public to welcome the tyrant. Says Socrates: "Extreme freedom can't be expected to lead to anything but a change to extreme slavery, whether for a private individual or for a city."

Adeimantus wants Socrates to explain what kind of man resembles the democratic city. In other words, he wants to know how "democratic man" comes to be and what happens to make this freedom loving man eventually beg for a tyrant. Socrates clarifies that the democratic man starts out as the son of an "oligarchic" father -- a father who is thrifty and self-disciplined. The father's generation is more concerned with wealth than freedom. This first generation saves, invests, and rarely goes in for conspicuous consumption.

The father's pursuit of wealth leaves him unwilling and unable to give attention to his son's moral development. The father focuses on business and finance and ignores the business of family. The son then begins to associate with "wild and dangerous creatures who can provide every variety of multi-coloured pleasure in every sort of way." These Athenian precursors of the hippies begin to transform the son's oligarchic nature into a democratic one. Because the young man has had no moral guidance, his excessive desire for "unnecessary pleasures" undermines "the citadel" of his soul. Because the "guardians" of the son's inner citadel -- truth, restraint, wisdom -- are absent, there is nothing within him to defend against the "false and boastful words and beliefs that rush up and occupy this part of him."

A 1960s revolution in the son's soul purges the last remaining guardians of moderation and supplants new meanings to old virtues: "anarchy" replaces freedom, "extravagance" replaces magnificence, and "shame-lessness" replaces courage. The young man surrenders rule over himself "to whichever desire comes along, as if it were chosen by lot." Here Socrates notes the essential problem when a free society becomes detached from any notions of moral virtue or truth: desires are chosen by "lot" instead of by "merit" or "priority."

For the son, the democratic revolution in his soul is complete. In this stage "there is neither order nor necessity in his life, but he calls it pleasant, free, blessedly happy, and he follows it for as long as he lives." Socrates gives a brief illustration of the young man's new democratic life:

Sometimes he drinks heavily while listening to the flute; at other times he drinks only water and is on a diet; sometimes he goes in for physical training; at other times, he's idle and neglects everything; and sometimes he even occupies himself with what he takes to be philosophy. He often engages in politics, leaping up from his seat and saying and doing whatever comes into his mind. If he happens to admire soldiers, he's carried in that direction, if money-makers, in that one.

In short, the young man has no anchor, no set of guiding principles or convictions other than his thirst for freedom. His life is aimless, superficial, and gratuitous. The spoiled lotus-eaters of his generation have defined themselves simply by mocking all forms of propriety and prudence. What's worse, as these Athenian baby-boomers exercise their right to vote, they elect "bad cupbearers" as their leaders. The new cupbearers want to stay in office so they give the voters whatever they desire. The public, according to Socrates, "gets drunk by drinking more than it should of the unmixed wine of freedom." Conservative politicians who attempt to mix the wine of freedom with calls for self-restraint "are punished by the city and accused of being accursed oligarchs."

As conservative politicians court suspicion so do conservative teachers and academics who stubbornly hold on to objective measurements of performance: "A teacher in such a community is afraid of his students and flatters them, while the students despise their teachers or tutors." Conservatism becomes unpopular just about everywhere, to a point at which even the elderly "stoop to the level of the young and are full of play and pleasantry, imitating the young for fear of appearing disagreeable and authoritarian."

The explosion of boundaries and limits extends even to national identity itself, so that resident aliens and foreigners "are made equal to a citizen."

The citizens' souls become so infected with freedom that they become excessively paranoid about any hint of slavery. But slavery comes to mean being under any kind of master or limit including the law itself. Says Socrates: "They take no notice of the laws, whether written or unwritten, in order to avoid having any master at all." That is, any kind of "hierarchy" in a democracy is rejected as "authoritarian." But this extreme freedom, according to Socrates, eventually enslaves democracy.

As the progressive politicians and intellectuals come to dominate the democratic city, its "fiercest members do all the talking and acting, while the rest settle near the speakers platform and buzz and refuse to tolerate the opposition of another speaker." There are "impeachments, judgments and trials on both sides." The politicians heat up the crowds by vilifying business and wealth and by promising to spread the wealth around. The people then "set up one man as their special champion" and begin "nurturing him and making him great."

The people's "special champion" however transforms from leader to tyrant. He "drops hints about the cancellation of debts and the redistribution of land" and continues to "stir up civil wars against the rich." All who have reached this stage, says Socrates, "soon discover the famous request of a tyrant, namely, that the people give him a bodyguard to keep their defender safe for them." The people give him this new security force, "because they *are* afraid for his safety but aren't worried at all about their own."

Socrates describes the early weeks of the new leader's reign:

"Won't he smile in welcome at anyone he meets, saying that he's no tyrant, making all sorts of promises both in public and in private, freeing the people from debt, redistributing land to them, and to his followers, and pretending to be gracious and gentle to all?"

After a series of unpopular actions, including stirring up a war in order to generate popular support, the leader begins to alienate some of his closest and most ardent advisers who begin to voice their misgivings in private. Following a purge of these advisors the tyrant attracts some of the worst elements of the city to help him rule. As the citizens grow weary of his tenure the tyrant chooses to attract foreigners to resupply his dwindling national bodyguard. The citizens finally decide they've had enough and begin to discuss rebellion.

At this point in the dialogue Adeimantus asks Socrates incredulously: "What do you mean? Will the tyrant dare to use violence against [the people] or to hit [them] if [they] don't obey? Socrates answers: "Yes - once he's taken away [the people's] weapons."

Thus ends Book VIII of Plato's *Republic*. I won't spoil the marvellous ending (Books IX and X) but I would like to spend a few moments drawing some conclusions about the overall message of this fascinating text and its relevance for 21st century Americans.

First, those of us who are incapable of self-mastery will always shamefully prostrate ourselves before messianic political leaders. The progressive left in America has spent countless generations destroying the guardians of the inner citadel: religion, family, parents, and tradition - in short, conservatism and limits. When people exhaust the financial and moral capital of previous generations (and future ones, as with the current stimulus bill) we will dutifully line up at the public trough, on our knees. Citizens capable of self-mastery will always choose to be left alone. In other words, they'll always choose limited government.

Second, freedom without limits paves the way to tyranny by undermining respect for the law. When politicians play fast and loose with the law it becomes easier for them and for the people to see special champions as alternative sources of rule. Today in America the objective basis for law is being attacked on campuses and even in law schools as too authoritarian and too insensitive to the subjective experiences and personal narratives of criminals. The SAT[26] and the British GCSE[27] exams have also been under assault for the same reasons. As Socrates warned: "extreme freedom will instil a paranoia about any kind of "master" including objective measurements of right and wrong, and of merit-

---

[26] Scholastic Aptitude Test
[27] General Certificate of Secondary Education (GCSE)

based forms of achievement. But when the citizens become enslaved to their vices they'll dutifully cry out for another kind of master."

Third, is the crucial role of education, which is the underlying theme of Plato's *Republic*. The ethos of American education has been for many decades saturated with a simple mantra: choice. What's worse, those few remaining educators who chant the old, Socratic mantra of "judgment" are vilified and harassed by the modern-day lotus-eaters[28] as hateful conservatives. Socrates predicted that all of this would happen in a democracy. But it is judgment not choice that enables a young person to erect a citadel in the soul. This eliminates the need for tyrants, and for bailouts too.

Finally, there is a question on the minds of many conservatives today: How does one convince the younger generations of Americans to distrust the growth of the State? Is it possible for Americans to recover the desire to be left alone in order "to realise our capacities and talents" as Eric Hoffer says?

---

[28] In Greek mythology, the lotus-eaters (Greek: λωτοφάγοι, translit. lōtophágoi) were a race of people living on an island dominated by the lotus tree, a plant whose botanical identity is uncertain. The lotus fruits and flowers were the primary food of the island and were a narcotic, causing the inhabitants to sleep in peaceful apathy. After they ate the lotus they would forget their home and loved ones, and only long to stay with their fellow lotus-eaters. Those who ate the plant never cared to report, nor return.
Figuratively, 'lotus-eater' denotes "a person who spends their time indulging in pleasure and luxury rather than dealing with practical concerns".

I've read that in Iran, many young people chafe at the pervasive despotism there, but when the burning desire for freedom threatens to boil over, the government in Tehran eases its restrictions on the use of personal satellite dishes. Electronic Soma[29] for the digital age.

THE TRANSGENDER

TSUNAMI

"Anybody who has ever taken even a rudimentary course in Gender Studies will know that there are literally no biological differences between men and women. Except in the case of trans people, who are born in the wrong body."

Titania McGrath (McGrath)

Social conservatives and millions of profoundly nurturing parents are increasingly asked to justify why they have decided to target

---

[29] Soma, the drug used widely by characters in Aldous Huxley's "Brave New World," symbolizes a replacement for religion in society. In this new world, soma allows people to escape from reality by thinking less critically. The novel, which was published in 1932, refers to the drug as having "all the advantages of Christianity and alcohol; none of their defects.

transgender youth as if they picked this issue because it polls well or some other such inanity.

Let me make it clear why this has become a concern. It is because in the USA, in 2007, had exactly one gender clinic, one.

Care to guess how many Gender Clinics exist in the USA today? There are now more than 300 registered paediatric Gender Clinics. In the USA, Planned Parenthood[30] gives out testosterone on a first visit. Depending on the state, it absolutely gives testosterone to minors. Planned Parenthood in Oregon gives it to 15-year-old girls on their own recognisance. They don't even need a parental note. Kaiser[31] dispenses it, also without parental consent or professional medical advice.

So for today's teens, whether they have real or typical gender dysphoria or not, testosterone is easily available. Double mastectomy, known as top surgery, is readily available. They do not need parental approval and they definitely don't need a therapists note.

OK, so let's talk about the transgender phenomenon. I'm going to start by walking through the major issues and claims about youth and adolescent gender transition. And we'll work our way to the big question, which is; how on earth did we get here?

---

[30] "Planned Parenthood is a trusted health care provider, an informed educator, a passionate advocate, and a global partner helping similar organizations around the world. Planned Parenthood delivers vital reproductive health care, sex education, and information to millions of people"...(sic)

[31] Kaiser Permanente is one of the United States largest "not-for-profit" health plans (sic). It makes billions of dollars in "excess" each year.

How did we get to a place in which we're all supposed to pretend that the only way you know that I'm a man is if I give you my pronouns? In Sweden today, women are now called "person with a Uterus". When did we give away all our decency and regard for biological definitions of sex and gender. How did we get to an America in which a 15-year-old in Oregon can begin a course of testosterone without her parents' permission? A lot of the answer, of course, comes from the hard left. But at least one part of the answer is conservative squeamishness about issues we'd rather not deal with at all. So let's begin by dealing with it.

WHAT IS GENDER DYSPHORIA?

Gender dysphoria, the severe discomfort in one's biological sex, is absolutely real. It's also exceedingly rare, typically afflicting roughly 0.01% of the population, and overwhelmingly males.

So roughly 1 in 10,000 males meaning, nobody you went to high school with. And it typically began in early childhood, ages two to four, little boys insisting, no, mommy, I'm not a boy. I'm a girl-- boys who were insistent, consistent, and persistent in this feeling that they were in the wrong body.

It is by all accounts excruciating. Many transgender adults, most of them biological males, describe the relentless chafe of a body that feels to them, all wrong. According to Abigail Shrier[32]; There are at least three separate issues to discuss around this complex and complicated subject.

1. There are the young kids who have this classic presentation of gender dysphoria, the majority of whom are male and would have naturally outgrown it on their own, and historically did. Others became what we used to call transsexual adults.

2. There is the social contagion currently spreading among adolescent girls, many of whom do not have typical gender dysphoria at all. This is a mental condition very close to eating disorders and self-harm. These serious and common conditions require professional assistance and intervention; not hormone treatments and surgery. It is a social and temporal aberration.

And third;

3. There are the activists who have already begun exploiting our confusion and our sympathies in order to invade women's protective spaces and destroy women's sports.[33]

They are all very different.

The young kids: Traditionally these were overwhelmingly little boys and if left alone, meaning with no intervention either to change their name and pronouns, what we now call social transitioning, and no

---

[32] Author of; Irreversible Damage: The Transgender Craze Seducing Our Daughters. 2020. Named a book of the year 2021 by the Economist and one of the best books of 2021 by the Sunday Times.

[33] *Shirer writes that there was a "sudden, severe spike in transgender identification" among teenagers assigned female at birth during the 2010s. She attributes this to a social contagion among "high-anxiety, depressive (mostly white) girls who, in previous decades, fell prey to anorexia and bulimia or multiple personality disorder".*

medical intervention, over 70% of these kids typically outgrew gender dysphoria on their own. Most would end up as gay men, and some would not. Some would not outgrow it and go on to be called what we used to call transsexuals.

Transsexuals were not people who used to pretend they were somehow really women or were always truly female.

They were just people who felt most comfortable presenting as female. Many transgender adults from our recent past, have told researchers and will tell you themselves that they know that people can tell that their biology is different. Their goal isn't so much to fool other people as it is to achieve a level of comfort with themselves. For many, that involves hormonal intervention and surgeries. Miss Shrier writes in her extraordinary book; "I've talked to many transexuals who say that hormones they took or the surgeries they underwent brought them a measure of peace. I can also tell you that they are generally holding down steady jobs and are leading good, productive lives."

But today, we don't just leave kids alone who say this and let the chips fall where they may, letting some kids outgrow their gender dysphoria and others to transition when they reach adulthood. Today we decide the moment a child seems not perfectly feminine or not perfectly masculine, today we say, "I know what! This is a trans kid."

We take them to a therapist or doctor, nearly all of whom practice so-called affirmative care, that is nearly all of whom have accepted that it is their job to immediately affirm or agree with the patient's self-diagnosis and to immediately help them medically transition. Teachers affirm young children in school, both by teaching the class that only they, the children, know their true genders, and encouraging kids to re-introduce themselves to the class with their new name and pronouns.

Therapists affirm and encourage minors down this path, and even pae-diatricians do. The typical next step for these kids, after changing their name and pronouns to their friends and classmates, is puberty blockers. Puberty blockers shut down the part of the pituitary that directs the re-lease of hormones catalysing puberty. The most common of these drugs is called Lupron, a drug that was originally used in the chemical castra-tion of sex offenders. To this day, it has never been FDA approved to halt healthy puberty. Now you might ask, why would any parent or doc-tor do this?

Why would anyone stop the puberty in a child, even a child with genu-ine gender dysphoria when that child would be highly likely to outgrow the gender dysphoria if left alone? Some say because it's traumatizing to let a child go through the puberty of the sex to which they don't wish to belong. The problem of this, of course, is that in many cases, puberty does seem to have helped children overcome their gender dysphoria.

There really is no satisfying answer to why someone would do this given that scientists have no way of predicting which children will out-grow the dysphoria on their own and which won't. But the argument that's made is that these kids can't wait. The suicide rates for the trans identified youth and trans adults are very high, the argument goes. So we need to get in there and start fixing them as soon and dramatically as possible. But unfortunately, there are no long-term studies that indicate that puberty blockers cure suicidality or even that they produce better mental health outcomes. There are not even good studies that show they are safe for this population long term, nor that they are reversible.

There's a big debate right now in the medical community about whether and to what extent the effects of stopping healthy puberty in adolescents is reversible if these kids later stop taking them. What we do know is that puberty blockers will block all the secondary sex characteristics, sexual maturation, and development of bone density from occurring.

We do know that because of the inhibition of bone density and other risks, doctors don't like to keep a child on puberty blockers for more than two years. We know that once a child's healthy puberty is arrested, placing her entirely out of step with her peers, this seems to guarantee that she will proceed to cross-sex hormones like testosterone.

"In recent studies, nearly 100% of kids who are put on puberty blockers proceed to cross-sex hormones." (Shrier) We know that if a child goes from puberty blockers to cross-sex hormones, that child will be infertile. She may also have permanent sexual dysfunction given that her sex organs never reached adult maturity, but she will certainly be infertile. So the claim that puberty blockers are safe and reversible for this population is not well founded. The claim that it's a neutral intervention, just a pause button, they say, without serious downsides is simply false. We wouldn't accept this level of glib salesmanship in any other area of medicine.

OK, so those are the kids who actually have gender dysphoria. For the nearly 100-year history of diagnosing gender dysphoria, these little kids were what we were talking about when we talked about gender dysphoria. But in the last decade that, thanks in large part to social media, there's been another population that claims to have gender dysphoria. This is a population that never before had gender dysphoria in any significant numbers. In fact, before 2007, there was no extant scientific literature on their having gender dysphoria at all - teenage girls. This is the phenomenon Brown University Public Health researcher Dr. Lisa Littman called "rapid onset gender dysphoria." It refers to a sudden spike in transgender identification among teen girls with no childhood history of gender dysphoria at all. Not only have the rates of these girls claiming trans identification risen dramatically in the US and all across the West - over 4,400% rise in teen girls presenting for gender treatment at the UK's national gender clinic, for instance but teenage girls are now the leading demographic of those claiming to have gender dysphoria.

What's going on?

The answer is social contagion, one more instance of teen girls sharing and spreading their pain. There's a long history of peer contagion with this demographic, of course. We know that anorexia and bulimia spread this way. We know that this demographic, teen girls, is in the midst of the worst mental health crisis on record with the highest rates of anxiety, self-harm, and clinical depression we've ever seen. We know that the population who tends to fall into social contagions is the same high-anxiety, depressive group of girls who struggle socially in adolescence and tend to hate their bodies. Add to that a school environment where you can achieve immediate valorisation and popularity by declaring a trans identity and, of course, the delicious temptation to stick it to mom.

Add further the great many trans social media influencers who can't wait to convince troubled teen girls that identifying as trans and starting a course of testosterone will cure all of their problems, and you have a very fast spreading social phenomenon. An increasing number of families of girls at top girls' schools that will attest that 15%, or 20%, or in one case 30% of the girls in their daughter's seventh grade class now identify as trans. When you see that, you're witnessing a social contagion in action. There is no other reasonable explanation. These teen girls are in a great deal of very real pain.

Almost all of them have dealt at some point with an eating disorder, or engaged in cutting, or have been diagnosed with other serious mental health comorbidities.

Now they're being allowed to self-diagnose with gender dysphoria by a medical establishment that's decided its job is merely to affirm and agree with these girls, a medical establishment that has, with regard to trans identified adolescents, effectively turned its doctors into life coaches.

Since Ms Shrier's book, Irreversible Damage, was published in June of 2020, more evidence than we ever could have imagined has come out indicating that this thesis is correct. You may not know the name Keira Bell. This is a young woman in the UK, very troubled in adolescence, who was rushed to transition in her teen years and came to regret it. She underwent double mastectomy and spent years on testosterone only to realize that her problem had never been gender in the first place. She sued the national gender clinic in England. Then back in December 2020, the High Court of Justice examined her case and the claim of similarly-situated plaintiffs, and she won. The Court examined the medical protocols applied to her; protocols identical to the ones we have in America.

The High Court of Justice was horrified.

It was absolutely appalled that a young girl had been allowed to consent to eliminating her future fertility and sexual function at an age when she could not have possibly gauged that loss.

She had begun transitioning at 15.

This case was called a landmark case in England. It was covered by The Times of London, The Economist, and even The Guardian. It was seen as a real condemnation of the effort to fast track so many young girls to transition. One of the things the Court noted was that the clinic had been unable to show any psychological improvement in the girls it had treated with transitioning hormones. If you didn't read about the landmark Keira Bell case in the American legacy media, well, that's because they decided to pretend it didn't happen, just as they continue to ignore or dismiss the stories of the thousands of de-transitioners.

These are young women who underwent medical transition and later regretted it and attempt to reverse course. A lot of these treatments are permanent, but they do what they can to try to reverse some of the effects. So in America, the teen trans phenomenon gets treated as a conservative issue, that is a political issue rather than a medical one. So perhaps the greatest medical scandal of this decade is dismissed as a conservative preoccupation. Finally, there's a third group of people we talk about when we talk about the transgender phenomenon. This is the group that seems to want to eradicate girls' and women's sports and protective spaces.

Many or most of these proponents are not transgender themselves, but they are activists and they are energized. They do seem to be winning. They promote dangerous bills like the Equality Act, now before the US Senate, which would make it impossible ever to distinguish between biological men and women, ever to exclude a biological male from a girls' sports team, or a scholarship, or a woman's protective space like locker rooms and prisons. They would do this based entirely on a male's self-identification. All that a violent male felon needs to do is announce his new pronouns and identity, and he becomes eligible to transfer into women's prison wherever such laws are found. They have these laws now in California and the state of Washington. As you might imagine, hundreds of biological male prisoners have already applied to transfer in. For this third group, it is not enough that we create a separate unisex bathroom while preserving a women's room for women.

It is not enough to have an open category for those trans identified athletes who do not wish to be stigmatized while preserving the girls' team for biological girls. It is not enough to keep a separate safe zone in a prison for those trans identified biological men who might be at risk in male prison. No, they are working to abolish all women's-only spaces. They want all men to be able to self-identify their way into them, and they want to do it right now. So these three groups are very different. You have the young children, some of whom do suffer with gender dysphoria. You have the adolescent girls, most of whom are caught in a social contagion. You have the activists who are using the other two groups to attack women and to advance their goal of chaos and social upheaval.

What these three have in common has nothing to do with real gender dysphoria. What they have in common is that they are all shrouded in gender ideology. Put another way, what they have in common is that they are all soaked in lies. Lies are told about the risks of the treatments we administer to young children, both to play down the very real dangers and to wildly exaggerate the degree to which we know medical transition to be a cure. Lies are told about the researchers and journalists who tried to report on the social contagion among teen girls in order to discredit that hypothesis or to stifle its revelation. Lies are told both about the inherent dangers of eradicating women's protective spaces and rights and to exaggerate the degree to which this is the only way to save a community from suicide.

The way to think about gender ideology is that it is a sibling of critical race theory. Critical race theory goes into schools to convince white kids that they bear the original sin of their skin colour. Gender ideology marches into those same schools and tells kindergartners; yes, they do this throughout the public school system in California beginning in kindergarten; to tell preschool children that there are a great many genders. While someone may have guessed at birth that you were a boy or a girl, only you know your true gender.

Critical race theory postulates that race is the most important feature of any person and that white people, existing as they do in a state of racial privilege, are not able to participate in a wide variety of discussions about our democracy.

Gender ideology tells women, which it calls cis women, that they are not entitled to their fear or their sense of unfairness as biological men invade their protective spaces and claim their trophies, and records, and scholarships. In fact, women and girls can't even use the English language to describe their problem since calling a trans woman biological male is an act of transphobic bigotry. Both of these invidious, mendacious dogmas have corrupted our schools, our universities, almost all of our legacy newspapers and magazines, the medical accrediting organizations, American Academy of Paediatrics, American Medical Association, American Psychiatric Association, the Paediatric Endocrine Society, and even our scientific journals.

Just to give you a sense of how far things have gone, about eight months ago, Ms Shrier was contacted by a member of the National Association of Science Writers. The NASW is an association of journalists with scientific backgrounds tasked with explaining scientific phenomena to the public. The member of the NASW who contacted her wanted her to know that a member of the online forum had been expelled for mentioning her book. She contacted the member, the person who mentioned her book, who had been expelled, Sean Scott. He apparently informed her that he hadn't even read the book. It just sounded interesting to him. He was immediately banned from the forum and labelled as transphobic.

I've read much the same thing from endocrinologists, and psychiatrists, and paediatricians, and scientific researchers who write around these issues. If they point out the risks of gender interventions, they struggle to get their research into journals. Very often, there are letters. to the editor pointing out flaws in studies touting all these interventions. Those letters aren't published. The funding goes to research that promotes gender transition and downplays the risks. There are phalanxes of young doctors now, many of them in paediatrics or child psychiatry, who believe their primary job is social justice. They don't hide this. They brag about it online every day. We are now starting to see this kind of thing put into practice. Perhaps America's most prestigious hospital, Brigham and Women's Hospital in Boston, recently announced that it would offer preferential care to patients based on race.

On questions of gender, we're seeing it with a mass celebration of transitioning treatments provided to young people by doctors who show an inexcusable complacency about the risks of these treatments. The Washington Post just last week (July 21, 2021) quoted some of these young doctors and claimed that it was a factual matter that puberty blockers are fully reversible. That was the quote. Puberty blockers are fully reversible, except that that's not something anyone can claim to know yet. They're certainly not psychologically reversible, and they may not be physically reversible either. We simply don't have the data yet. So we are seeing this startlingly quick corruption of medicine and science. And it's a symptom of a larger "woke" corruption of society.

So I never say, and will never say, trans women are women. This is a dangerous lie. It's a lie which, when promoted in public, leads to unjust and even dangerous consequences for women and girls. When we lie in public, we usher in all kinds of consequences, the obliteration of women's protective spaces and the destruction of women's and girls' athletics.

Rejecting lies; sorry, parroting these lies is not mere courtesy, whatever proponents say. It's the cowardly surrender of women's welfare as a sacrifice to the woke gods, and it's wrong.

In the public sphere, the lie is the harm. It does damage to our ability to communicate, to comprehend each other. It makes it impossible to object in the face of unfairness and cruelty. If, "a trans girl really is just a kind of girl after all," there is no basis for objecting to a 17-year-old boy who handily beat all the girls on the track team.

Now, why are the trans activists doing this? Why would a teacher tell her class of kindergartners that only they know their true gender? What could possibly be the justification for telling small boys that they might really be girls and telling small girls that they might really be boys? The biggest hint I got to the answer came from researching the stories from many detransitioners. Remember, these are young women who underwent transition and then later regretted it. Again and again, they write that while they were transitioning, they were angry, they were sullen, and they were politically radical. They very often cut off their families. They were coached in this by transgender influencers online. They rushed toward their new glitter families. You'll often see gender confused people among the ranks of Antifa or at Black Lives Matter rallies. Having turned against their families of origin, they are easy prey for those who recruit revolutionaries.

Put another way, the chaos is the point. Just as the point of critical race theory is to turn the American people against one another, so the point of gender ideology is to stop the formation of stable families, the building blocks of societal life. This is not the goal of all transgender adults, but it is the goal of gender ideology and the transgender movement, namely the creation of a new victim class eager to join the revolution.

So what do we do about this?

How do we push back on the onslaught of gender ideology?
First, we must oppose the indoctrination of children in gender ideology. There is absolutely no good reason for it. It does very real harm. You

can absolutely insist that all children treat each other kindly without indoctrinating an entire generation in gender confusion. Second, in public we must speak up, and we must speak the truth. Always, wherever we find ourselves, at work, whatever we do, we must refuse to recite the lies.

If conservatives are to confront these issues, we know we must know something about them. We must overcome our squeamishness. We must clearly distinguish, for instance, between transgender citizens, many of whom are wonderful, and an ideological movement which seeks to warp our children and wreck our families.

This is a movement that would turn our children against themselves because its advocates know there is no greater harm, there's no greater horror to a parent, there is no quicker way to bring society to its knees than by prompting our children to do irreversible damage to themselves.

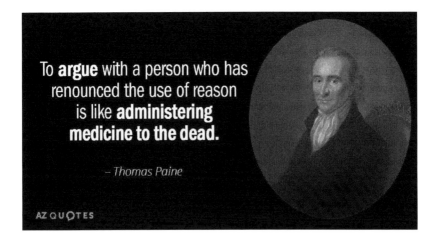

To **argue** with a person who has renounced the use of reason is like **administering medicine to the dead.**

– Thomas Paine

AZ QUOTES

The people who've been pushing this ideology have a big head start on us, perhaps by a decade. But they have awakened a sleeping giant.

Abigail Shrier finished a powerful speech at Hillside College with the following, powerful words: "The success of my book, the fact that I was invited to speak to you today, and the state legislators that are now debating these issues testify that a cultural battle is at last being fought. We cannot afford to lose. These are our kids and grandkids. Our future literally depends on our winning this."

MONTY PYTHON: LIFE OF BRIAN

I've always loved this following scene from this iconic and very funny, if a little dated, movie. I just wonder how long it will be before this movie will join the ranks of banned and shamed literature, comedy, satire and commentary that wokeists will no longer allow. It's up to us to preserve the human condition and the right to freedom of expression. Not to mention preserving scientific truth, gender reality and common sense.

Reprinted with permission:
http://www.montypython.50webs.com/Life_of_Brian.htm

JUDITH: I do feel, Reg, that any Anti-Imperialist group like ours must reflect such a divergence of interests within its power-base.

REG: Agreed. Francis?

FRANCIS: Yeah. I think Judith's point of view is very valid, Reg, provided the Movement never forgets that it is the inalienable right of every man--

STAN: Or woman.

FRANCIS: Or woman... to rid himself--

STAN: Or herself.

FRANCIS: Or herself.

REG: Agreed.

FRANCIS: Thank you, brother.

STAN: Or sister.

FRANCIS: Or sister. Where was I?

REG: I think you'd finished.

FRANCIS: Oh. Right.

REG: Furthermore, it is the birthright of every man--

STAN: Or woman.

REG: Why don't you shut up about women, Stan. You're putting us off.

STAN: Women have a perfect right to play a part in our movement, Reg.

FRANCIS: Why are you always on about women, Stan?

STAN: I want to be one.

REG: What?

STAN: I want to be a woman. From now on, I want you all to call me 'Loretta'.

REG: What?

LORETTA: It's my right as a man.

JUDITH: Well, why do you want to be Loretta, Stan?

LORETTA: I want to have babies.

REG: You want to have babies?

LORETTA: It's every man's right to have babies if he wants them.

REG: But... you can't have babies.

LORETTA: Don't you oppress me.

REG: I'm not oppressing you, Stan. You haven't got a womb! Where's the foetus going to gestate?! You going to keep it in a box?

LORETTA: crying

JUDITH: Here! I-- I've got an idea. Suppose you agree that he can't actually have babies, not having a womb, which is nobody's fault, not even the Romans', but that he can have the right to have babies.

72

FRANCIS: Good idea, Judith. We shall fight the oppressors for your right to have babies, brother. Sister. Sorry.

REG: What's the point?

FRANCIS: What?

REG: What's the point of fighting for his right to have babies when he can't have babies?!

FRANCIS: It is symbolic of our struggle against oppression.

REG: Symbolic of his struggle against reality.

The Transgender Flag; blue, pink, white, pink, blue.

ORIGINS OF "WOKE"

"WOKE" IN THE UK

The new "woke" seems to have originated in the 1940's in African American Vernacular English (AAVE) to refer to being 'woken up to' or alert to issues around racial injustice and inequity. As you can see, this "woke" is significantly more narrow in its definition and meaning than the original usage of the word from 1762.

Following the inauguration of the new US president, Joseph Robinet Biden, in January of this year (2021), Boris Johnson (Prime Minister of the UK) was asked if Mr Biden was "woke".

The prime minister answered that there was "nothing wrong with being woke", but that it was "important to stick up for your history, your traditions and your values, the things you believe in".
So in other words, nothing at all like "Woke".

The word "woke" is difficult to get away from in the media and popular culture these days, but before the Black Lives Matter[34] movement, it was barely known in the UK despite having been used in the US throughout the early 2000s.

---

[34] https://www.independent.co.uk/topic/black-lives-matter

"Woke" is currently used by the political left to refer to progressiveness and social justice, while those on the political right have weaponised it as a way to denigrate those who disagree with their beliefs.

But where did the word come from, and how did it arrive at this point?

ORIGIN OF THE WORD "WOKE"

The phrase "woke" and to "stay woke" is not new — it began appearing in the 1940s and was first used by African Americans to "literally mean becoming woken up or sensitised to issues of justice", says linguist and lexicographer Tony Thorne.

Mr Thorne, a visiting consultant at King's College London, told *The Independent*[35] that; "the word is rooted in African American Vernacular English (AAVE), and was used in American street and youth culture for a long time." [pws: *Just what is a long time Mr Thorne?*]

In 1971, the phrase was used in a play by American playwright Barry Beckham titled Garvey Lives!, in which he wrote: "I been sleeping all my life. And now that Mr Garvey done woke me up, I'm gon' stay woke. And I'm gon' help him wake up other black folk."

It also entered popular culture thanks to singer Erykah Badu, who used the phrase "I stay woke" in her 2008 song Master Teacher. David

---

[35] https://www.independent.co.uk/news/world

Stovall, a professor of African-American studies at the University of Illinois, Chicago, told the New York Times that Ms Badu's use of the phrase meant "not being placated, not being anaesthetised".

It started becoming a politicised word in 2014, after the death of Michael Brown in Ferguson, Missouri, sparked the Black Lives Matter (BLM) movement. It was re-coined by Congress Woman, Maxine Waters in her violent and racist appeal to the far, radical left of the Democrat Party and carried with it the connotation of anti-male, anti-white, ant-family, anti-cis gender, anti-Republican, anti-democracy, anti-constitution, anti-anything that isn't Black, Trans, Gay, Lesbian and at least 1000 other ridiculous caveats and labels. In fact anti anything that the extreme left says it is.

Congressman Maxine Waters (D California): The face of "woke" hatred (image AAP)

Woke was largely unknown in the UK until the BLM movement, but in the 2000s it was a popular word used by young people in America, especially in black communities," said Mr Thorne.

"In a land without learning, only the fools believe"
Toto: I will remember, 1995

THE TWISTING OF "WOKE"

It was only in 2017 that the word "woke" was added to the Oxford English Dictionary, and was defined as "being 'aware' or 'well-informed' in a political, social or cultural sense".

It evolved into an all-encompassing term to describe leftist political ideology, used as a "shorthand for people on the extreme left" to signal progressiveness, but weaponised by those on the right as a "sneering, jeering dismissive term" to denigrate those who did not agree with their beliefs, said Mr Thorne.

Recommended video
Bill Burr's controversial SNL monologue divides viewers[36]

Like phrases before it such as *politically correct, social justice warrior* and *cancel culture*; "woke" has become a toxic term used by alt-right and politically conservative groups to insult people on the left.

Our My Thorne has more to say on the usage of the word:
"People who are woke simply can't use the word anymore," he explained. "It's been appropriated, co-opted and toxified by the alt-right and right-wing speakers. Those who are woke can still talk about empathy and compassion and social justice, but I think they've had to

---

[36] https://bit.ly/Bill-Burr-SNL

abandon the neat, snappy slang words and go back to explaining what they really believe."

HOW IS THE WORD USED NOW?

The word "woke" may have previously been a convenient, single-word summation to encompass ideologies centred around social justice for people on the political left. But for those on the right, it was "very exotic, a short sharp word... that sounds quite percussive and almost shocking when you don't know what it means".

"It's very easy to latch on to, like the word 'snowflake', which when weaponised by the right, has the same sort of resonance. You haven't been able to use it in a positive way because it was picked up by the right to be used for ridicule and dismissal," he said.

People who actually identify as "woke" no longer use the word to describe themselves, preferring to use more complex language such as "empaths" or "social justice" instead of "woke" due to its current negative connotations.

The word "liberal" is another word that has become unusable by people who actually identify as such, as it can be used as or perceived as a slur.

Such terms are known in the US as "skunk terms", explains Mr Thorne, phrases that are increasingly used in such toxic ways that they "stink" too much to be used in their original contexts.

IS THERE ANOTHER WORD TO REPLACE "WOKE"?

Not at the moment, according to Mr Thorne. People who are woke have mostly abandoned the term because it is being used with "malicious intent" by those with opposing views, but no similar slang word has surfaced in its place.

"When the word "woke" was being used by woke people, it wasn't a word they obsessed about, so perhaps it is inconvenient but they wouldn't mind much about having to abandon it," he said.

In a debate on social media, Mr Thorne found that people who were progressive did not want to be "condemned with a lazy, casual slur like that".

He thinks the next word could be more academic or scientific, but whatever it is, "we do need a vocabulary that progressives can use, they deserve to have that", he said.

However, any word that crops up to replace "woke" could easily be co-opted once again by those with opposing ideologies."

"I do fear that the same process of terms appearing and then being hijacked and weaponised might be likely to happen again," said Mr Thorne.

Oh really Mr Thorne? I confess that I find myself thinking that our My Thorne, consultant, is perhaps just a tiny bit blind when it comes to this particular subject. From my position, I think it's absolutely fabulous when consultants into academia or politics find it necessary to use their privileged platforms for virtue signalling of this nature. Personally, I would prefer it if they could stay objective or at the very least, professional and honest in their comments and "research".

However, this is precisely why I felt the need to tackle this subject. Researchers, academics, students, teachers, politicians and public servants from all over the political spectrum seem to have totally lost the concept of independence, consultation and compromise. It has become a world of confrontation and criticism; and when that type of discourse becomes the norm, then we have truly betrayed our society, our past and our future.

PART 2: PURE "WOKE" INSANITY

As I got older, I excelled at all academic subjects, except for biology, physics, chemistry, economics, history, religious studies, computing and mathematics. I quickly realised that it was not due to 'failure' on my part, but rather that these fields of study are patriarchal constructs that perpetuate white privilege. My adolescent self was intuitively mistrustful; my low grades were doubtless a valiant act of subconscious self-sabotage. As Professor Rochelle Gutiérrez from the University of Illinois has pointed out, 'on many levels, mathematics itself operates as Whiteness'. Indeed, the Ku Klux Klan were once known to set fire to plus signs in order to intimidate their victims.

McGrath, Titania. (McGrath)

CLASSICAL MUSIC AS IMPLICIT WHITE SUPREMACY

The preferred Jewish epithet to throw at White people who have the temerity to do what Jews do routinely: openly advocate for their ethnic interests, has long been; "White Supremacist". This hackneyed label has always been utterly beside the point: whether Whites are superior to non-Whites has no logical bearing on the moral legitimacy of White people defending their collective interests. Having said this, everyone is well aware that the achievements of all people in countless cultural and scientific domains. In some fields, such as science, architecture and literature, the multitude of achievements of white people surpass those of other groups, and

81

can objectively be regarded as "a superior contribution." Another conspicuous example is the Western musical tradition. To do so is not racist , it is factual. We can certainly say that in the fields of mathematics, geometry and astrology during the 7th century, Islam dominated the fields and did so for nearly 1000 years. The superiority of Western classical music is so decisive one could almost rest the argument for the superiority of Western culture on it alone. There exists a hierarchy in the world of sound, as in other phenomena. Noise occupies the lowest rung in this hierarchy; it is an undifferentiated mass of sound in which no distinction exists. The earliest type of music, such as that of Australian Aboriginal culture, most closely corresponds to noise and rhythm. Western classical music, by contrast, exists on a totally different plane because it apprehends sound in the most highly differentiated way possible. It is the farthest from noise and most fully exploits the inherent potential of the world of sound.

How well this potential is apprehended and developed can lead to Bach's inimitable counterpoint, the extraordinary tonal architecture of Beethoven's symphonies, Bruckner's sonic cathedrals — or to banging on a hollow log with a stick. Besides stimulating pleasure in audiences, great classical music has an unrivalled capacity to shed light on our ontological predicament and connect aesthetic experience with the transcendental. Goethe once noted, with reference to Bach's great fugues, where as many as five separate lines of musical argument are simultaneously sustained, that "it is as though the eternal harmony has a conversation with itself." Only Western classical music, I would argue, can create this sublime impression.

To point out the foregoing is to trigger rage from anti-White commentators who huff that it has "long been an argument of white supremacists, Nazis, Neo-Nazis, and racial separatists that 'classical music,' the music of 'white people,' is inherently more sophisticated, complicated, and valuable than the musical traditions of Africa, Asia, South America, or the Middle East, thus proving the innate superiority of the 'white race.'" The problem with this assessment, aside from denying the very existence of the White race, is the inability to demonstrate (or even attempt to demonstrate) that Western classical music is *not* inherently more sophisticated, complicated, and yes valuable, than other musical traditions.

That classical music stands as a glaring (and galling) testament to the pre-eminence of European high culture (and implicitly of the race overwhelmingly responsible for it), was evident in the reaction to a speech President Trump gave in Poland in 2017. The speech, praising Western civilization, included the line "we write symphonies." Jonathan Capehart, a columnist at *The Washington Post*, fumed: "What on Earth does that have to do with anything? In that one line, taken in context with everything else Trump said, what I heard was the loudest of dog whistles. A familiar boast that swells the chests of white nationalists everywhere." For Anthony

Tomassini of *The New York Times*, Trump's point, extolling the "richness, history and, indeed, the superiority of Western culture," was "all too clear and dismaying," Alex Ross, Jewish music critic for the *New Yorker*, found "ludicrous and sinister" Trump's "implication that some cultures are incapable of creating symphonies," a sentiment that, he maintained, should have "stirred bad memories."

I find it absolutely abhorrent that in the 21st century, it is not possible to take even a modicum of pride in the western (white) traditions such as Greek drama and philosophy, Roman architecture and roads and of course the aqueduct, Religion and religious art including music; really there is 2000 years of history of art, literature, science, religion and music. All of it as a direct result of the (*awful, racist, demonic*) white people, their history, culture and intelligence. The very fact that simply by saying these things, our "woke" friends decry the whole history and scream out "what about all the other cultures that have given us fantastic art"… well you "woke" morons, of course they still exist and just as the protagonists are righteously proud of their cultural heritage, It is high time that white people are permitted to enjoy their cultural heritage again. I cannot understand why this has to be a zero-sum game. *"You celebrating whitey is racist; us celebrating brown and black people is glorious."* More on this to come.

AS INSUFFICIENTLY DIVERSE

As well as decrying as deeply offensive the invocation of classical music to praise Western civilization (and thus White people), commentators routinely bemoan the lack of "diversity" in the genre. According to Jewish music critic Greg Sandow, the "problem of racial diversity in classical music has long been the elephant in the room," and he labels "ugly" the fact that classical music, "in practice pretty much a lily-white art," claims "special privileges (lavish funding, school programs devoted to it) in an age of growing diversity." Rather than simply reflecting the divergent preferences and aptitudes of different racial groups, the under-representation of Black and Brown people in Western orchestras (and their audiences) is inevitably ascribed to White racism. Black screenwriter Candace Allen, the ex-wife of conductor Sir Simon Rattle, branded the British classical music world "racist," claiming a "combination of discrimination and lack of exposure to classical music at an early age meant Blacks were unlikely to make it to the concert hall (in the audience or on stage), and when they did, "their sense of alienation made the experience not one to be repeated."

I absolutely reject this statement from Miss Allen. What a ridiculous comment especially that her husband is a world-renowned conductor and is perfectly placed to actually inform his wife of the facts. Auditions are closed and screened. I only include the comments here in the interest of balance and to highlight the issue that plagues our orchestras and concert goers, that is *Virtue Signalling[37]*. When a very privileged white female decries her husband's profession for its lack of diversity and does so publicly, it is obviously a ploy to head off any overt criticism of her or her husband by broadcasting out to the world just how "woke" they are. There are no suggestions forthcoming of how to fix the perceived racist industry, just screams and declarations that its racist and horrible. Unbelievable.

According to this conception, an insidious White supremacist conspiracy keeps the classical repertoire dominated by the music of dead White men performed by living White men, and prevents Black and Brown people from succeeding in the genre. For the "White supremacist" social order to be maintained, Raymond Arsenault insists, "Blacks had to know their place, and the world of popular music was one of the places where they allegedly belonged." While the "relativist revolution begun by anthropologist Franz Boas and others had already eroded the presumption of black inferiority," in the Western world of public opinion and culture, "the time-honoured shibboleths[38] of white-supremacy held sway."[i] One of these "shibboleths" was that:

---

[37] Virtue signalling is the conspicuous communication of moral values and good deeds. The term has negative connotations as it is commonly used to denote virtuous actions and statements are motivated by a desire for social status and self-satisfaction.

[38] A shibboleth is any custom or tradition, usually a choice of phrasing or even a single word, that distinguishes one group of people from another.

"Mastery of classical technique required superior intelligence, discipline, and years of training. The world of classical music was the province not only of natural talent but of cultivated genius. Here the barriers to black achievement were thought to be both cultural and physiological. Conventional wisdom held that blacks did things naturally and impulsively without much thought or deliberation. Classical music, by contrast, was intellectual, highbrow, and European in origin. As such, it was deemed inappropriate for African Americans three or four generations removed from the jungles of Africa. Black success in the world of classical music would be tantamount to beating whites at their own game, something that could not be tolerated or even contemplated in white supremacist circles. It would represent an affront to white sensibilities, upsetting expectations based on multiple layers of observation and socialization."

The White supremacist conspiracy to thwart Black and Brown achievement in classical music purportedly extends to musical education where, in the most commonly used theory textbooks in the United States, only 1.63% of musical examples come from non-White composers. This is problematic for Linda Shaver-Gleason because studying a particular piece "reaffirms its canonical status; enshrining it in a textbook is deeming it *worthy of study*." Constantly referencing White composers "reinforces the idea that they're the ones who deserve the most respect, as if to say, 'Marvel at the many *techniques* Mozart used so *perfectly*!" Ethan Hein, a (presumably Jewish) doctoral fellow in music education at NYU, decries the stubbornness of music teachers in teaching "European-descended" classical music over that of "music descending from the vernacular traditions of the African diaspora." Orienting music education towards the European classical tradition, an "implicit racial ideology," is, he declares, "insidious" in its "affirmations of Whiteness."

While White people are chastised for "appropriating" the cultures of non-White groups, the notion they should be allowed to maintain cultural and artistic institutions reserved exclusively for their own racial group is considered anathema. The Vienna Philharmonic came under attack in the 1990s for its failure to embrace the new ideological and moral imperatives of increased racial and gender diversity. One commentator condemned the orchestra for "its consistently racist and sexist hiring practices," dismissing as "clearly absurd" claims made by representatives of the orchestra that it performs an essentially European art-form and thus should be composed of White men. Dieter Flury, a flutist for the orchestra, opined at the time that:

"From the beginning we have spoken of the special Viennese qualities, of the way music is made here. The way we make music here is not only a technical ability, but also something that has a lot to do with the soul. The soul does not let itself be separated from the cultural roots that we have here in central Europe. And it also doesn't allow itself to be separated from gender. So if one thinks that the world should function by quota regulations, then it is naturally irritating that we are a group of white skinned male musicians that perform exclusively the music of white skinned male composers. ... If one establishes superficial egalitarianism, one will lose something very significant. ... something produced by a superficial understanding of human rights would not have the same standards."

Music writer Stefan Aune insists the European domination of classical music cannot be attributed to advantageous genetic endowments possessed on average by White people, and has "no patience for individuals or institutions harbouring antiquated beliefs about the superiority of White-European performers or composers." Ignoring all the data proving the existence of significant racial differences, he ascribes such beliefs to "racism and a fundamentally incorrect view of musical history." The European domination of classical music has, he insists, everything to do with "cultural inequalities" and nothing to do with inborn characteristics:

"In the last analysis, racial and gender inequalities throughout the history of classical music are a question of access rather than innate ability. Individuals like [mulatto composers] Chevalier de Saint George, Samuel Coleridge-Taylor and George Bridgetower erode the argument that classical music is an exclusively white-European cultural enterprise. They show that individuals from any background can succeed in the western musical tradition, and they also show that the western musical tradition is not nearly as culturally homogeneous as many would argue."

The composers identified here are remembered solely because they were non-White; not because of the excellence of their compositions. Rather than being excluded from the classical repertory because of their music's relative lack of quality and popularity, Linda Shaver-Gleason believes they are victims of the aforementioned White supremacist conspiracy which has "intentionally suppressed" their music "in the service of a narrative of white, specifically German, cultural supremacy (because, alas, that too is part of Western culture)."

CONSTRUCTING BEETHOVEN AS BLACK

Even the romantic idea of the composer-genius is regarded as an element of this conspiracy to keep Western classical music a Whites-only field. For Shaver-Gleason, "The conflation of 'genius' and 'white man' means that no minority will be viewed as a real genius, and hence not a real composer." Given Beethoven's status as the archetypal musical genius, it is unsurprising that aggrieved Blacks have, since the early twentieth century, attempted to propagate the myth that Beethoven had some African ancestry. The basis for this spurious claim was the composer's somewhat swarthy complexion, and the fact a part of his family traced its roots to Flanders, which was for a period under Spanish monarchical rule. Because Spain had a longstanding historical connection to North Africa through the Moors, a degree of blackness supposedly trickled down to the great composer.

The myth was eagerly disseminated by Jamaican "historian" Joel Augustus Rogers (1880–1966) in works like *Sex and Race* (1941–44), the two-volume *World's Great Men of Color* (1946–47), *100 Amazing Facts About the Negro* (1934), *Five Negro Presidents* (1965), and *Nature Knows No Color Line* (1952). Rogers, whose intellectual rigor was basically non-existent, claimed that Beethoven; in addition to Thomas Jefferson, Johann Wolfgang von Goethe, Robert Browning, and several popes, among others, were genealogically African and thus Black. Despite being thoroughly debunked, the myth still lingers in contemporary culture: in 2007 Nadine Gordimer published a short story collection called _Beethoven Was One-Sixteenth Black: And Other Stories_[39]. The determination, contrary to all evidence, to make Beethoven Black is, of course, a desperate attempt to make the composer and his oeuvre a glorious symbol of Black accomplishment.

Shaver-Gleason warns such efforts are self-defeating, merely serving to treat the Western canon as fundamental and all other styles as deviations from this norm, thus reinforcing "the notion that of classical music as a universal standard and something that everyone should aspire to appreciate." Trying to make Beethoven Black and desperately scouring the historical records for examples of non-Whites who wrote symphonies is to accept "a white-centric perspective that presents symphonies as the ultimate human achievement in the arts." Black musicologist Philip Ewell agrees, and advocates "overthrowing the existing structure and building a new one that would accommodate non-white music _a priori;_ no reaching for 'inclusion' necessary because non-white composers would already be there." One Black music writer endorses this stance, and resents that the waltzes of Johann Strauss Jr. are regarded as part of the body of superior classical music, while the music of James Brown, "the Godfather of Soul", is regarded as mere entertainment.

---

[39] https://bit.ly/black-beethoven

THE EAST ASIAN AFFINITY FOR WESTERN CLASSICAL MUSIC

Curiously, the alleged White supremacist conspiracy that allegedly prevents Blacks and Browns from succeeding in classical music doesn't have the same effect on East Asians – the one non-White group that likes performing and listening to classical music. A survey[40] of Asian-Americans aged 18–24 found 14 percent attended a classical concert in the preceding year, more than any other demographic in that age group. Asian attendance rates match or surpass the national average up through the 45–54 age range. The younger the classical music audience gets, the more Asian it becomes.

Unlike non-White groups affronted by claims to the superiority for Western classical music, East Asians are under no illusion about the inferiority of their own musical tradition when compared to European art music. This acknowledgement lies at the heart of why East Asian parents are so enthusiastic for their children to play and appreciate the genre. As Amy Chua acknowledges in her widely publicized (and criticized) *Battle Hymn of the Tiger Mother* (Chua):

"That's one of the reasons I insisted [my two daughters] do classical music. I knew that I couldn't artificially make them feel like poor immigrant kids. ... But I could make sure that [they] were deeper and more cultivated than my parents and I were. Classical music was the opposite of decline, the opposite of laziness, vulgarity, and spoiledness. It was a way for my children to achieve something I hadn't. But it was also a tie-in to the high cultural tradition of my ancestors [Chua is proud to be descended in the direct

---

[40] https://bit.ly/Asiansurvey

male line from Chua Wu Neng, Imperial Astronomer to a 17th-century emperor]. ... To me, the violin symbolized respect for hierarchy, standards, and expertise. For those who know better and can teach. For those who play better and can inspire. And for parents. It also symbolized history. The Chinese never achieved the heights of Western classical music – there is no Chinese equivalent of Beethoven's Ninth Symphony – but high traditional music is deeply entwined with Chinese civilization."

Chua is married to a Jew and recalls her stereotypically Jewish mother-in-law (a "progressive" art critic) being opposed to her grandchildren learning the violin; suggesting they learn Indonesian gamelan percussion instruments as more in keeping with the multicultural zeitgeist of the contemporary West. To back her case, she noted how French composer Claude Debussy had been captivated by gamelan music which helped inspire shimmering impressionistic masterpieces like *L'apres midi d'un faun*. Chua is distinctly unimpressed with this line of argument:

"Personally, I think Debussy was just going through a phase, fetishizing the exotic. The same thing happened to Debussy's fellow Frenchmen Henri Rousseau and Paul Gauguin who started painting Polynesian natives all the time. A particularly disgusting variation of this phenomenon can be found in modern-day California: men with Yellow Fever, who date only Asian women – sometimes dozens in a row – no matter how ugly or which kind of Asian. For the record, Jed [her husband] did not date any Asian women before me. Maybe the reason I can't appreciate gamelan music, which I heard when we visited Indonesia in 1992, is that I fetishize difficulty and accomplishment. ... Gamelan music is mesmerizing because it is so simple, unstructured, and repetitious. By contrast, Debussy's brilliant compositions reflect complexity, ambition, ingenuity, design, conscious harmonic exploration — and yes, gamelan influences, at least in some of his works. It's like the difference between a bamboo hut, which has its charm, and the Palace of Versailles." (Chua)

Debussy first heard Indonesian gamelan music at the Paris Exhibition in 1889 and possibly again at the same event in 1900. In his biography of Debussy, musicologist Stephen Walsh notes that while it's common to talk about the influence of the gamelan on Debussy's compositions, it merely accentuated existing aspects of his style:

"He did not need the gamelan to teach him the pentatonic scale, the whole-tone scale or modalism. They were already part of his language. Insofar as this contact with the oriental musical mind helped release him from the toils of Wagnerism and, worse, the [conservatively-inclined] Conservatoire, the truth is that it did so only in part and quite gradually."

East Asia has produced countless young technical virtuosos, but their nimble fingers and admirable work ethics are often not matched by the emotional depth required for the successful interpretation of nineteenth-century Romantic repertoire. Chinese film director, and classical music fan, Chen Kaige, hopes Western classical music can educate an intensely materialistic and collectivist Chinese people in spirituality and individualism. "One of the biggest differences between Chinese and Western culture," he points out, "is that we don't have religion. We don't worship anything. Western classical music has elements of love and forgiveness that come from religion. Chinese music is very intellectual, very exotic, but there is no love. You don't feel warm after you listen to it."

APPRECIATION OF CLASSICAL MUSIC CORRELATED WITH INTELLIGENCE

The East Asian affinity with Western classical music is perhaps not surprising given that appreciation of the genre has been correlated with higher intelligence.

Evolutionary psychologist Satoshi Kanazawa posits that more intelligent people populate concert halls because they're more likely to respond to purely instrumental works. By contrast, people across the intelligence spectrum seem to enjoy vocal music. Kanazawa's Savanna-IQ Interaction Hypothesis[41] predicts highly intelligent people are more likely to adopt evolutionarily novel preferences and values. According to this theory, they are better able to comprehend, and thus enjoy, novel stimuli. Vocal music predated sonatas by many millennia, so, in evolutionary terms, purely instrumental music is a novelty — which, according to Kanazawa's theory, means highly intelligent people are more likely to appreciate and enjoy it.

Studies support Kanazawa's theory, finding clear preferences for instrumental musical genres among those who score higher on intelligence tests. Controlling for age, race, sex, education, family income, religion, current and past marital status and number of children, more intelligent people are more likely to prefer instrumental music than less-intelligent people. A 2019 Croatian study[42] confirmed these findings, showing that people with lower intelligence preferred music with lyrics, rather than complex orchestrations. 467 teenagers performed a non-verbal intelligence test and were then asked to rank musical genres in order or preference. Those who recorded the highest IQ scores displayed a clear preference for

---

[41] https://bit.ly/music-IQ
[42] https://bit.ly/croation-study

instrumental music. On the other extreme, preference for rap music is significantly negatively correlated with intelligence.

The Savanna-IQ Interaction Hypothesis helps to explain why Black people (as a low-IQ group) are generally repulsed by classical music, and why it has been used successfully as a crime prevention mechanism in racially-diverse cities around the world. Neurologists note[43] that certain types of music work as a crime deterrent because of people's neurobiological responses to things they don't enjoy or find unfamiliar. When people hear music they like, it stimulates dopamine production and puts them in a better mood. But when people dislike the music, their brains respond by suppressing dopamine production — souring their mood and making them avoid it.

[43] https://bit.ly/music-in-the-brain

Mass non-White immigration into Western nations has ensured that, for a growing percentage of their populations, classical music holds little or no appeal. Classical music audiences in the United States and other Western nations are contracting: according to a National Endowment for the Arts survey, in the early twenty-first century, the percentage of American adults who attended at least one classical music event dropped from 11.6 to 8.8 in just ten years.

Non-White immigration to the West was always unpopular with existing White populations who were assured it posed no long-term threat to their demographic and cultural dominance. This was always a lie: changing the demographics and culture of the West (in Jewish interests) was the core motivation for these policies. With the Great Replacement now well underway, even White people who enjoy a White art form – like classical music – are regarded by some as engaging in an activity that should make them feel "uncomfortable." One White commentator, for example, laments that "we don't seem uncomfortable enough" when "sitting in the concert halls of Europe and America's cosmopolitan cities in a usually very white audience listening to a usually very white orchestra."

African-American writer Teju Cole is similarly perplexed that White people who enjoy hearing White musicians playing White music don't feel more uncomfortable: "It never ceases to surprise me" he notes, "how easy it is to leave the hybridity of the city, and enter into all-white spaces, the homogeneity of which, as far as I can tell, causes no discomfort to the whites in them." Jewish music critic Greg Sandow likewise finds offensive that, "in a diverse culture, classical music stands out (on the whole) as strikingly white, and that even many white people, especially younger ones ... look at classical music, and feel (whether they put it in words or not, or even if they don't consciously know they think this) that something isn't quite right, that this isn't the country they live in." The solution to this problem, according to Fred Bronstein, the Jewish former director of the St. Louis Symphony, is for future classical music audiences to be "much more diverse than we can even dream of today. And audiences will only become truly diverse when the performers on our stages are diverse."

Hang on there, Fred. Clearly you have not heard of *cultural appropriation*.[44] A white person playing jazz is apparently abhorrent due to the cultural appropriation by the performer of an art form from outside their own culture. One of the principal dogmas of Wokeism is of course calling people out for cultural appropriation. So black and brown people playing white man's music would be exactly the same thing according to the truly "woke". Personally I love the fact that practically all orchestras today have a very high number of Asian musicians in them. In fact as a young musician growing up in

[44] Cultural appropriation is the adoption of an element or elements of one culture or identity by members of another culture or identity.

"White" Canberra, I both performed with and rehearsed with Asian, Indian and Aboriginal kids in the orchestras and choirs that I performed with. I don't perform middle eastern music as I have not grown up with it and do not understand it structures and scales. In fact I do not properly understand the cultures that have produced it despite spending several years studying Indonesian Gamelan to try to develop an understanding for this varied musical genre. Sadly, I suspect that even this opportunity would be declined to a white boy from Canberra today, because of the ridiculous claim of cultural appropriation. Learning something or adopting a style of clothing that you love should not be branded in this way. If this is true then all immigrants should stop wearing jeans and shirts (the emblems of the wicked western society) and adopt their own national dress for everyday wear. But guess what, they won't because they are more comfortable in the clothes of the society they have chosen to join.

It is not racist to do so and we must stop labelling everything in our society with a racial brush and stop viewing the world through a racial lens. It is harmful, it is divisive and it is a vial form of racism itself. The following rubbish is a quote that I found online and is fully unattributed. Possibly because it is so vial and racist. Again, I publish here in the interest of balance and opposite views to my own.

Classical music, like other aspects of Western culture, has been a casualty of the anti-White diversity mania that now infests Western intellectual life. The Cultural Marxist critique of classical music wallows in bad faith arguments and cognitive dissonance: Western classical music is nothing exceptional, yet cannot be invoked to praise White people because this necessarily implies the inferiority of other races; a White supremacist conspiracy thwarts Black and Brown achievement in the genre, but it utterly fails to prevent East Asian interest and success; Black composers have written symphonies (and, indeed, Beethoven himself was Black (sic)), yet the Western classical music tradition is inherently White supremacist and needs radical deconstruction.

Ultimately, the reason invoking classical music to laud White people is so keenly resented by anti-White intellectuals is because the gap in civilisational attainment it underscores is an embarrassing affront to regnant egalitarian assumptions. Classical music is one of the crowning glories of Western civilisation, and White people have every right to take pride in their race's achievements in the genre, and to cite these achievements as motivation for pro-White activism.

CLASSICAL MUSIC: AN ALTERNATE TRUTH

In any case, there are *plenty* of composers of colour who write and wrote classical music, and many of my readers will be quick to cite names such as : William Grant Still, Florence Price, Toru Takemitsu, Unsuk Chin, Alberto Ginastera, Clarence Cameron White…and that's just a small fraction of the non-white classical composers!

Florence Price, whose music is experiencing a revival due to a recent discovery of her lost works.

Still, these composers were born after 1880, making it seem like non-white composers is a relatively recent trend, as though there was a moment when people of colour suddenly learned how to write music in a European style. More accurately, the events of the twentieth century impacted white-dominated establishments in such a way that they became more willing to acknowledge non-white contributors to the Fine Arts. Considering conservative discourse over the past century, it's all too easy to dismiss multiculturalism as modernism and something that "ruined" art music, rather than accepting modernism as the milieu that all music of the twentieth century participated in or reacted to.

Particularly in America, the rise of African-American composers in the late nineteenth century is often tied to narratives of post-Civil War freedoms as well as a visit from canonical composer Antonín Dvořák—suggesting that America needed a European master to reveal and direct black Americans' potential for high art music.

But there have been non-white composers even *before* the nineteenth century, and some of them were—get this!—*European*. That's right: Europe is not one big block of whiteness, and pretty much never has been—at least since the purported beginning of the Western music tradition, c. 800. Europe has so many ancient cities built by and for trade with Asia and Africa. As goods shuffled around, so did people. Europe has had a diversity of skin colours for centuries, despite white-supremacist narratives that mythologize Medieval Europe as a continent of pure   whiteness.

One of the most famous pre-1800 non-white composers is Joseph Bologne, Chevalier de Saint-Georges (1745-99). He was born in the Caribbean to a black slave mother with a French aristocrat and plantation owner as his father. That father sent him to Paris as a child for his education, where he earned a reputation as an exceptional fencer and soldier as well as a violinist and composer. Bologne is often called "The Black Mozart," a nickname that reinforces the primacy of white canonical composers—as though Bologne can only be conceptualized in terms of a more "history-worthy" contemporary.

In fact, Bologne knew Mozart; they met in Paris while Mozart visited in 1778. At that point, Bologne was an established musical celebrity, known for his violin concertos as well as his leadership of *Le Concert des Amateurs*, a highly regarded orchestra. Mozart, then 22 years old, was still struggling to secure a steady position.

"The Black Mozart"? Could Mozart lead a regiment of soldiers? Mozart isn't even worthy of being called "The White Joseph Bologne"!

Even though Wikipedia says Bologne is "best remembered as the first classical composer of African ancestry," I recently came across an article on Vincente Lusitano, a non-white composer and music theorist born in Portugal in 1522! Like Bologne, he was mixed-race, with a black mother and Portuguese father.

The article provides an explanation for why Lusitano's African heritage would be overlooked: "Europe's musicologists would later try and detach him from his mixed background and would regard him as white." Such whitewashing affects other composers as well, though not always to the same degree. For instance, Ludwig van Beethoven is often depicted as having pale skin, despite being described by his contemporaries as bearing a "strong resemblance to a mulatto", because *of course* the greatest representative of the German musical canon could *not* have had dark skin.

(There has been a persistent myth that Beethoven was black, but research confirms that he wasn't.)

I bring up historical examples because I believe it is important to recognize that cultural diversity isn't just some recent "fad," or some progressive plot to weaken Western culture. It *is* Western culture, woven into the fabric of society through the centuries. Multiculturalism is not new. And just as I believe in highlighting woman composers from earlier eras to challenge narratives of women being eventually granted the ability to compose by patriarchal society, I point to these composers as proof that people of colour have been creating classical music for far longer than most people realize, but their music has been intentionally suppressed in the service of a narrative of white—specifically German—cultural supremacy (because, alas, that too is part of Western Culture). Clearly, people of all races, religions, genders, and sexualities can create classical music!

And yet…

Maybe this is the wrong debate to be having. Maybe we're focused on the wrong thing. Maybe by proclaiming that, "Classical music is for and by everyone!", we reinforce the notion of classical music as a universal standard and something that everyone should aspire to appreciate. The matter of who writes the symphonies accepts a white-centric perspective that presents symphonies as the ultimate human achievement in the arts.

I hadn't fully considered these implications until I read a paper by Philip Ewell* which he delivered at the Post-Truth conference. During the presentation, he pointed out that, of the most common theory textbooks used in American higher education, only 1.63% of the musical examples come from non-white composers. This oversight has a profound impact on how music students regard non-white composers. Studying a particular piece reaffirms its canonical status; enshrining it in a textbook is deeming it *worthy of study*. Over-representing the "great" composers reinforces the idea that they're the ones who deserve the most respect, as if to say, "Marvel at the many *techniques* Mozart used so *perfectly!*"

*September 2018, "Music and Musicology in the Age of Post-Truth," University College Dublin. Paper entitled, "Was Heinrich Schenker a White Supremacist, and If So, What Then?"

REFERENCES:

i.   Raymond Arsenault, *The Sound of Freedom: Marian Anderson, the Lincoln Memorial, and the Concert That Awakened America* (New York: Bloomsbury, 2009), 8
ii.   *Ibid.*, 75
iii. Amy Chua, *Battle Hymn of the Triger Mother* (London: Bloomsbury, 2011), 22.
iv.   *Ibid.*, 40-41.
v.   Stephen Walsh, *Debussy: A Painter in Sound* (London: Knoph Doubleday, 2018) 211.
vi.   Teju Cole, *Open City* (New York: Random House, 2011) 252.

Black Beethoven? ... maybe not.

CRITICAL RACE THE-ORY: FOR DUMMIES

The following is adapted from a lecture delivered at Hillsdale College on March 30, 2021.

Critical race theory is fast becoming America's new institutional orthodoxy. Yet most Americans have never heard of it - and of those who have, many don't understand it. It's time for this to change. We need to know what it is so we can know how to fight it.

In explaining critical race theory, it helps to begin with a brief history of Marxism. Originally, the Marxist Left built its political program on the theory of class conflict. Marx believed that the primary characteristic of industrial societies was the imbalance of power between capitalists and workers. The solution to that imbalance, according to Marx, was revolution: the workers would eventually gain consciousness of their plight, seize the means of production, overthrow the capitalist class, and usher in a new socialist society.

During the 20th century, a number of regimes underwent Marxist-style revolutions, and each ended in disaster. Socialist governments in the Soviet Union, China, Cambodia, Cuba, and elsewhere racked up a body count of nearly 100 million of their own people. They are remembered for their gulags, show trials, executions, and mass starvations. In practice, Marx's ideas unleashed man's darkest brutalities.

By the mid-1960s, Marxist intellectuals in the West had begun to acknowledge these failures. They recoiled at revelations of Soviet atrocities and came to realize that workers' revolutions would never occur in Western Europe or the United States, where there were large middle classes and rapidly improving standards of living. Americans in particular had never developed a sense of class consciousness or class division. Most Americans believed in the American dream—the idea that they could transcend their origins through education, hard work, and good citizenship.

But rather than abandon their Leftist political project, Marxist scholars in the West simply adapted their revolutionary theory to the social and racial unrest of the 1960s. Abandoning Marx's economic dialectic of capitalists and workers, they substituted race for class and sought to create a revolutionary coalition of the dispossessed based on racial and ethnic categories.

Fortunately, the early proponents of this revolutionary coalition in the U.S. lost out in the 1960s to the civil rights movement, which sought instead the fulfillment of the American promise of freedom and equality under the law. Americans preferred the idea of improving their country to that of overthrowing it. The vision of Martin Luther King, Jr., President Johnson's pursuit of the Great Society, and the restoration of law and order promised by President Nixon in his 1968 campaign defined the post-1960s American political consensus.

But the radical Left has proved resilient and enduring - which is where critical race theory comes in.

WHAT IS IT?

Critical race theory is an academic discipline, formulated in the 1990s, built on the intellectual framework of identity-based Marxism. Relegated for many years to universities and obscure academic journals, over the past decade it has increasingly become the default ideology in our public institutions. It has been injected into government agencies, public school systems, teacher training programs, and corporate human resources departments in the form of diversity training programs, human resources modules, public policy frameworks, and school curricula.

There are a series of euphemisms deployed by its supporters to describe critical race theory, including "equity," "social justice," "diversity and inclusion," and "culturally responsive teaching." Critical race theorists, masters of language construction, realize that "neo-Marxism" would be a hard sell. *Equity*, on the other hand, sounds non-threatening and is easily confused with the American principle of *equality*. But the distinction is vast and important. Indeed, equality - the principle proclaimed in the Declaration of Independence, defended in the Civil War, and codified into law with the 14th and 15th Amendments, the Civil Rights Act of 1964, and the Voting Rights Act of 1965 - is explicitly rejected by

109

critical race theorists. To them, equality represents "mere non-discrimination" and provides "camouflage" for white supremacy, patriarchy, and oppression.

In contrast to equality, equity as defined and promoted by critical race theorists is little more than reformulated Marxism. In the name of equity, UCLA Law Professor and critical race theorist Cheryl Harris has proposed suspending private property rights, seizing land and wealth and redistributing them along racial lines. Critical race guru Ibram X. Kendi[45], who directs the Centre for Antiracist Research at Boston University, has proposed the creation of a federal Department of Antiracism. This department would be independent of (i.e., unaccountable to) the elected branches of government, and would have the power to nullify, veto, or abolish any law at any level of government and curtail the speech of political leaders and others who are deemed insufficiently "antiracist."

One practical result of the creation of such a department would be the overthrow of capitalism, since according to Kendi, "In order to truly be antiracist, you also have to truly be anti-capitalist." In other words, identity is the means and Marxism is the end.

An equity-based form of government would mean the end not only of private property, but also of individual rights, equality under the law,

---

[45] Ibram Xolani Kendi is an African American author, professor, anti-racist activist, and historian of race and discriminatory policy in America. Author of: "How to be an Antracist".

federalism, and freedom of speech. These would be replaced by race-based redistribution of wealth, group-based rights, active discrimination, and omnipotent bureaucratic authority. Historically, the accusation of "anti-Americanism" has been overused. But in this case, it's not a matter of interpretation—critical race theory prescribes a revolutionary program that would overturn the principles of the Declaration and destroy the remaining structure of the Constitution.

HOW IT WORKS

What does critical race theory look like in practice? Earlier this year, I read a series of reports focused on critical race theory in the federal government. The FBI was holding workshops on intersectionality theory. The Department of Homeland Security was telling white employees they were committing "microinequities" and had been "socialized into oppressor roles." The Treasury Department held a training session telling staff members that "virtually all white people contribute to racism" and that they must convert "everyone in the federal government" to the ideology of "antiracism." And the Sandia National Laboratories, which designs America's nuclear arsenal, sent white male executives to a three-day re-education camp, where they were told that "white male culture" was analogous to the "KKK," "white supremacists," and "mass killings." The executives were then forced to renounce their "white male privilege" and write letters of apology to fictitious women and people of colour.

111

This year, Christopher F. Rufo[46] produced another series of reports focused on critical race theory in education in the United States. In Cupertino, California, an elementary school forced first-graders to deconstruct their racial and sexual identities, and rank themselves according to their "power and privilege." In Springfield, Missouri, a middle school forced teachers to locate themselves on an "oppression matrix," based on the idea that straight, white, English-speaking, Christian males are members of the oppressor class and must atone for their privilege and "covert white supremacy." In Philadelphia, an elementary school forced fifth-graders to celebrate "Black communism" and simulate a Black Power rally to free 1960s radical Angela Davis from prison, where she had once been held on charges of murder. And in Seattle, the school district told white teachers that they are guilty of "spirit murder" against black children and must "bankrupt [their] privilege in acknowledgement of [their] thieved inheritance."

When I say that critical race theory is becoming the operating ideology of our public institutions, it is not an exaggeration; from the universities to bureaucracies to k-12 school systems, critical race theory has permeated the collective intelligence and decision-making process of

---

[46] Founder and director of Battlefront, a public policy research center. He is a graduate of Georgetown University and a former Lincoln Fellow at the Claremont Institute for the Study of Statesmanship and Political Philosophy. As executive director at the Documentary Foundation, he has directed four films for PBS, including most recently America Lost, which explores life in Youngstown,Ohio, Memphis, Tennessee, and Stockton, California. He is also a contributing editor of City Journal, where he covers topics including critical race theory, homelessness, addiction, and crime.

American government, with no sign of slowing down - and it is spreading throughout other western democracies from Canada to the UK and Europe to Australia. It seems that teaching white kids that they are awful and teaching black kids that they are permanently oppressed by the white kids seems to be the racist model du jour all over the planet.

This is a revolutionary change. When originally established, these government institutions were presented as neutral, technocratic, and oriented towards broadly-held perceptions of the public good. Today, under the increasing sway of critical race theory and related ideologies, they are being turned against the American people. This isn't limited to the permanent bureaucracy in Washington, D.C., but is true as well of institutions in the states, even in red states, and it is spreading to county public health departments, small Midwestern school districts, and more. This ideology will not stop until it has devoured all of our institutions.

RESISTANCE IS FUTILE

Thus far, attempts to halt the encroachment of critical race theory have been ineffective. There are a number of reasons for this.

First, too many Americans have developed an acute fear of speaking up about social and political issues, especially those involving race. According to a recent Gallup poll, 77 percent of conservatives are afraid to share their political beliefs publicly. Worried about getting mobbed on social media, fired from their jobs, or worse, they remain quiet, largely ceding the public debate to those pushing these anti-democratic and violently racist ideologies. Consequently, the institutions themselves become monocultures: dogmatic, suspicious, and hostile to a diversity of opinion. Conservatives in both the federal government and public-school systems have told me that their "equity and inclusion" departments serve as political offices, searching for and stamping out any dissent from the official orthodoxy.

Second, critical race theorists have constructed their argument like a mousetrap. Disagreement with their program becomes irrefutable evidence of a dissenter's "white fragility," "unconscious bias," or "internalized white supremacy." I've seen this projection of false consciousness on their opponents play out dozens of times in my research. Diversity trainers will make an outrageous claim - such as "all whites are intrinsically oppressors" or "white teachers are guilty of spirit murdering black children" - and then when confronted with disagreement, they adopt a patronizing tone and explain that participants who feel "defensiveness" or "anger" are reacting out of guilt and shame. Dissenters are instructed to remain silent, "lean into the discomfort," and accept their "complicity in white supremacy."

Third, Americans across the political spectrum have failed to separate the premise of critical race theory from its conclusion. Its premise—that American history includes slavery and other injustices, and that we should examine and learn from that history—is undeniable. But its revolutionary conclusion—that America was founded on and defined by racism and that our founding principles, our Constitution, and our way of life should be overthrown—does not rightly, much less necessarily, follow.

Fourth and finally, the writers and activists who have had the courage to speak out against critical race theory have tended to address it on the theoretical level, pointing out the theory's logical contradictions and dishonest account of history. These criticisms are worthy and good, but they move the debate into the academic realm, which is friendly terrain for proponents of critical race theory. They fail to force defenders of this revolutionary ideology to defend the practical consequences of their ideas in the realm of politics.

POLITICAL ENGAGEMENT

No longer simply an academic matter, critical race theory has become a tool of political power. To borrow a phrase from the Marxist theoretician Antonio Gramsci, it is fast achieving "cultural hegemony" in most of our public institutions around the world. More and more, it is driving the vast machinery of the state and society. If we want to succeed in opposing it, we must address it politically at every level.

Critical race theorists must be confronted with and forced to speak to the facts. Do they support public schools separating first-graders into groups of "oppressors" and "oppressed"? Do they support mandatory curricula teaching that "all white people play a part in perpetuating systemic racism"? Do they support public schools instructing white parents to become "white traitors" and advocate for "white abolition"? Do they

115

want those who work in government to be required to undergo this kind of re-education? How about managers and workers in corporate America? How about the men and women in our military? How about every one of us?

There are three parts to a successful strategy to defeat the forces of critical race theory: governmental action, grassroots mobilisation, and an appeal to principle, honesty and integrity.

We already see examples of governmental action. Last year, a relevant report about the injustices of CRT led President Trump to issue an executive order banning critical race theory-based training programs in the federal government. President Biden rescinded this order on his first day in office, but it provides a model for governors and municipal leaders to follow. This year, several state legislatures have introduced bills to achieve the same goal: preventing public institutions from conducting programs that stereotype, scapegoat, or demean people on the basis of race. And I have organized a coalition of attorneys to file lawsuits against schools and government agencies that impose critical race theory-based programs on grounds of the First Amendment (which protects citizens from compelled speech), the Fourteenth Amendment (which provides equal protection under the law), and the Civil Rights Act of 1964 (which prohibits public institutions from discriminating on the basis of race).

DEFEATING THE "WOKE" AGENDA

On the grassroots level, a multiracial and bipartisan coalition is emerging to do battle against critical race theory. Parents are mobilizing against racially divisive curricula in public schools and employees are increasingly speaking out against Orwellian re-education in the workplace. When they see what is happening, Americans are naturally outraged that critical race theory promotes three ideas - race essentialism, collective guilt, and neo-segregation - which violate the basic principles of equality and justice. Anecdotally, many Chinese-Americans have told me that having survived the Cultural Revolution in their former country, they refuse to let the same thing happen here.

In terms of principles, we need to employ our own moral language rather than allow ourselves to be confined by the categories of critical race theory. For example, we often find ourselves debating "diversity." Diversity as most of us understand it is generally good, all things being equal, but it is of secondary value. We should be talking about and aiming at *excellence*, a common standard that challenges people of all backgrounds to achieve their potential. On the scale of desirable ends, excellence beats diversity every time.

Similarly, in addition to pointing out the dishonesty of the historical narrative on which critical race theory is predicated, we must promote the true story of western civilisations. A story that is honest about injustices in British and American history, but that places them in the context of our nations high ideals and the progress we have made towards realising them. Genuine British / American history is rich with stories of achievements and sacrifices that will move the hearts of all - in stark contrast to the grim and pessimistic narrative pressed by critical race theorists.

Above all, we must have courage—the fundamental virtue required in our time. Courage to stand and speak the truth. Courage to withstand epithets. Courage to face the mob. Courage to shrug off the scorn of the elites. When enough of us overcome the fear that currently prevents so many from speaking out, the hold of critical race theory will begin to slip. And courage begets courage. It's easy to stop a lone dissenter; it's much harder to stop 10, 20, 100, 1,000, 1,000,000, or more who stand up together for the principles of all western democracies, values which are being destroyed and eroded by unrestrained Wokeism. This leads me nicely into the next chapter where we shall discuss the influence of Marxism on "Woke" ideology and Wokeism as a new religion of hate.

As I got older, I excelled at all academic subjects, except for biology, physics, chemistry, economics, history, religious studies, computing and mathematics. I quickly realised that it was not due to 'failure' on my part, but rather that these fields of study are patriarchal constructs that perpetuate white privilege.

My adolescent self was intuitively mistrustful; my low grades were doubtless a valiant act of subconscious self - sabotage. As Professor Rochelle Gutiérrez from the University of Illinois has pointed out, 'on many levels, mathematics itself operates as Whiteness'. Indeed, the Ku Klux Klan were once known to set fire to plus signs in order to intimidate their victims.

Titania McGrath *(McGrath)*

TALKING ABOUT RACE IN THE USA

This truly ridiculous and highly racist poster was installed at the Smithsonian National Museum of African American History and Culture on 15th July, 2020. I know that it's too small to read so I will transcribe the full text. If any of this makes any sense at all to you, please, do not hesitate to let me know. I am at a loss to understand how this type of messaging does anything for race relations or even for mutual respect and understanding. It's a disgrace.

To be perfectly clear, the racial traits[47] listed on this poster, paid for by US taxpayers, is a list of all things that are supposed to be bad about Whiteness and White Culture. So

---

[47] **a:** a distinguishing quality (as of personal character) curiosity is one of her notable *traits*
b: an inherited characteristic

the only possible conclusion is that Blacks and African American people DO NOT exhibit or value these apparent cultural features or traits.

Some key identifying characteristics of "whiteness" the federal museum explains, include possessing a "master and control nature," "aggressiveness and extroversion," "heavy value on ownership of goods, space, property," a taste in "steak and potatoes; 'bland is best,'" and "no tolerance for deviation from single god concept," so be sure to watch out for these signs when interacting with others to steer clear of white people.

ASPECTS AND ASSUMPTIONS OF WHITENESS AND WHITE CULTURE IN THE UNITED STATES

"White dominant culture, or whiteness, refers to the ways white people and their traditions, attitudes and ways of life have been normalized over time and are now considered standard practices in the United States. And since white people still hold most of the institutional power in America, we have all internalized some aspects of white culture; including people of color (sic)."

Rugged Individualism:
• The individual is the primary unit
• Self-reliance
• Independence & autonomy highly valued + rewarded
• Individuals assumed to be in control or their environment. "You get what you deserve"

Family Structure:
• The nuclear family: father, mother, 2.3 children is the ideal
social unit

- Husband is breadwinner and head of household Structure
- Wife is homemaker and subordinate to the husband
- Children should have own rooms. be independent

Emphasis on the Scientific Method

- Objective, rational linear thinking
- Cause and effect relationships
- Quantitative Emphasis

History

- Based on Northern European immigrants' experience in the United States
- Heavy focus on the British Empire
- The primacy of Western (Greek, Roman) and Judeo-Christian tradition

Protestant Work Ethic

- Hard work is the key to success
- Work before play
- "If you didn't meet your goals, you didn't work hard enough"

Religion

- Christianity is the norm
- Anything other than Judeo - Christian tradition is foreign
- No tolerance for deviation from single god concept

Status, Power & Authority

- Wealth = worth
- Your job is who you are
- Respect authority

- Heavy value on ownership of goods, space, property

Future Orientation

- Plan for future
- Delayed gratification
- Progress is always best
- "Tomorrow will be better"

Time

- Follow rigid time schedules
- Time viewed as a commodity

Aesthetics

- Based on European culture
- Steak and potatoes; "bland is best"
- Woman's beauty based on blonde, thin - "Barbie"
- Man's attractiveness based on economic status, power, intellect

Holidays

- Based on Christian religions
- Based on white history & male leaders

Justice

- Based on English common law
- Protect property & entitlements Competition
- Intent counts

Competition

- Be #1
- Win at all costs
- Winner/loser dichotomy

- Acton orientation
- Mater and control nature
- Must always "do something" about a situation
- Aggressiveness and Extroversion
- Decision-Making
- Majority rules (when Whites have power)

Communication

- "The King's English" rules
- Written tradition
- Avoid conflict, intimacy
- Don't show emotion
- Don't discuss Personal life
- Be polite

Yep, that was all published by the NMAAC. As an indication of everything that's wrong about the white people and their culture. It wasn't in some extreme left scandal rag. It was published by the National Museum for Black People?? WTF??

Who runs that place? I am both shocked and a little flattered, that some racist moron thinks that these attributes are White and by postulation are not attributes of Black People. The KKK would be absolutely delighted. I'm absolutely certain that you will find this poster in all their huts or dens or nests, or whatever those low-lives gather in. Talk about the far left shooting itself in the foot.

Reprinted here for you edification and knowledge, is the text of the Washington Times from July 17, 2020.

The "Aspects and Assumptions of Whiteness in the United States" poster, part of the museum's "Talking About Race" series, was apparently intended to be critical of "white culture," but wound up being slammed as condescending and unfair to Black people for ascribing a multitude of positive traits to "whiteness."

YouTube host The Officer Tatum, a Black supporter of President Trump, ripped the museum for the graphic, calling it "racist" and an example of "the bigotry of low expectations for Black people."

"Why in the world would the African-American museum put out this document?" he asked in a Thursday video. "Simply allude to the fact that every great quality that you ever could imagine is only white people, like Black people have no good qualities. That's what this article is saying."

Yep...that is definitely what the poster is saying.

I am extremely glad that my family and I, don't live in the Divided States.

PART 3: WOKEISM, THE RELIGION: DOGMA OF HATE

John McWhorter, professor of linguistics, comparative religion, music history, and Americana at Columbia University has been pointing out (since at least 2015) that Woke anti-racism is a religion. McWhorter says, "When someone attests to his white privilege with his hand up in the air, palm outward . . . the resemblance to testifying in church need not surprise. Here, the agnostic or atheist American who sees fundamentalists and Mormons as quaint reveals himself as, of all things, a parishioner."

Wokeism satiates the religious cravings of the human spirit for people who have rejected conventional expressions of theistic worship. It has therefore become the current orthodoxy in the academic world and the official   religion   of   secular   society.

It has also become a kind of plaything for evangelicals who crave the world's admiration and approval—and who don't mind dabbling in syncretism. This is a frivolous and dangerous experiment, however, because no one who holds any real evangelical convictions can ever be truly Woke. Too many of Wokeism's cardinal tenets flatly contradict biblical principles. The truly Woke are militantly pro-abortion; devoted to the LGBTQIAAPQFLCIO+ agenda, rabid socialists, and high-handed secularists. Pure Wokeism is openly hostile to any whiff of evangelicalism.

Plus, Woke religion has a very insular creed. Soul liberty is antithetical to their fundamental convictions. They have a deep and abiding hatred for every worldview, idea, or person that challenges any point of their authorized credo. Indeed, to challenge Wokeism on any point or at any level whatsoever is deemed damnable heresy. Wokeism ironically fosters this extreme illiberalism[48] in the name of "tolerance and diversity."

Wokeism is as narrow-minded as any brand of fundamentalism; and getting more narrow every day. Every article of faith must be formally affirmed and faithfully adhered to. A catalogue of insider jargon signals other adherents that you too are Woke. But there are forbidden words that must be carefully avoided on pain of excommunication. And the list of taboo expressions is constantly being revised and expanded, so you must stay conversant with the approved vocabulary or risk being publicly shamed and shunned.

In addition to the strict cardinal dogmas, Wokeism has its own sacraments and rituals, high priests, saints, and martyrs—even a kind of hymnology. The flavour of Woke rhetoric is homiletical rather than scholarly; it's a sermonic appeal to deep emotions, utilizing personal testimony and a carefully-crafted narrative (the Woke mythology) rather than statistics.

It's an odd religion; teaching people to nurse grudges, cast blame, cultivate ill will against whole people groups, and deepen that personal sense of resentment. But it is nonetheless fully religious in character, for all the reasons noted.

The push to spread Woke doctrines therefore has all the characteristics

---

[48] opposed to liberal principles; restricting freedom of thought or behavior.

of a religious campaign; a crusade to win converts by any means possible. Conversion conveys a moral standing that non-converts (the uncooperative, unwashed, unWoke) don't have. It's a limited veneer of virtue that offers a provisional reprieve—nothing like full forgiveness. (More on that later.) But it entitles the penitent to join the Woke in heaping full-throated condemnation on the *un*Woke.

To a devotee of Wokeness, being *un*Woke is tantamount to being a rank heathen or an evil infidel. They see Wokeness not merely as a matter of politics; it is the **only** righteous worldview, and it **must** be embraced with pure religious fervour. Indeed, Woke anti-racism has quite literally become a point of religious doctrine so important that *even in the minds of the kinda-Woke evangelicals* it has upstaged and eclipsed abortion as the number one moral crisis in America and across the globe.

Wokeism is a nasty religious cult. Its votaries routinely declare people guilty for the sins of others, elicit rote confessions, and then refuse to offer absolution. They define sin mainly (if not entirely) as a horizontal offense—but not necessarily even a *personal* offense. You are guilty mainly for what your ancestors may have done. And even if your ancestors were themselves poor subsistence farmers who never oppressed anyone, if other members of your ethnic group did, you are made to bear the guilt for that. Guilt is therefore a corporate responsibility, apportioned differently to different ethnicities. In itself, a racist doctrine.

If you don't have the right kind of victim status or skin colour, it would be utterly foolish for you even to *think* of asking for forgiveness. Still, you *must* confess the guilt you bear by kneeling and reciting the prescribed confession. And if you don't do this, your refusal to genuflect on command will mark you as a fascist. The fact that you dissent from the received opinion intensifies the criminality you inherited when you were born into the wrong ethnic group. Preachers of the Woke doctrines will do everything they can to make sure you are shunned by polite society. Apologize publicly and you will merely be mocked (and subjected to endless re-indoctrination). But if you remain stubbornly **un-**Woke, those who are Woke will scold and harass you publicly, relentlessly, trying to get you fired from your job. Or worse.

On the other hand, if you are a cop, a civic leader, or a Christian, kneeling and accepting the Woke credo will do nothing to make you any less worthy of public contempt and censure.

After all, this is a religion that has no doctrine of atonement, no concept of forgiveness, and no possibility of real redemption. It almost total dogma is dividing people on the basis of race, gender, sexual preference and skin colour. It is a dogma of hatred and division. A religion that has its own saints and even a version of ex-communication, although they call it cancel culture, its own High Priests and even its own corruption and deceit and crimes against children. It is, in every way, a modern religion. Donations to BLM and Antifa are even tax free in the USA.

The recent BLM and Antifa demonstrations and riots made clear that no matter how frequently they use the word, *reconciliation* is not the real goal of Wokeism.

In short, the Woke worldview is impossible to blend with gospel truth, and the inevitable drift, will take today's wanna-be-Woke evangelicals exactly where the social gospel of Walter Rauschenbusch took the mainline denominations in the twentieth century: into rank theological liberalism and unbelief.

The notion that the gospel can be improved by blending it with Wokeism is sheer folly anyway. The Woke worldview is rooted in secularism; and arguably, Marxism. Its central claims and distinctive jargon are taken not from Scripture but from secular political discourse. It is a canon of doctrine deliberately designed to provoke conflict, prolong resentment, and foster bitterness between different ethnicities. It encourages people to be offended by things that never actually happened to them; while blaming others for sins they did not actually commit. It doles out guilt and shame rather than grace and redemption. Though it is promoted by people who say they oppose ethnic strife, it is a blatantly racist worldview, condemning entire ethnic groups for sins that were committed generations ago by people long dead.

All of that, hits at the heart of religions message of forgiveness, grace, oneness in God, and unity in the church. It is as anti-Christian, and anti every other Abrahamic religion or cult, and faithful followers of these ***should*** recognize that.

The High Priests of Wokeism: Nancy Pelosi, Chuck Schumer and their peons.

"WOKE" WORD SALAD

WHITE FRAGILITY, TOXIC MASCULINITY, THE CISHET[49] DILEMMA, MALE FRAGILITY, INTERSECTIONALITY AND OTHER MYTHS.

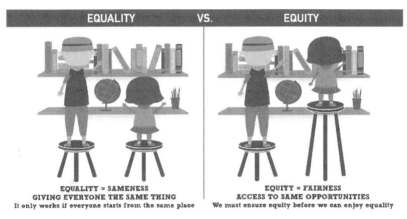

Equality and Equity are not the same. Equality means treating everyone the same and with equal opportunities for all. In "woke" speak, however;
"All people are equal but some are more equal than others". This they like to call equity. It is in, fact, a maxim off Marxism and adopted by the "Woke" to imply if you can afford better than someone else, good luck to you.
Paraphrased from "Animal Farm" Orwell, George (Secker and Warburg, London, England, 1945)

---

[49] An abbreviation of cis-gendered or cissexual heterosexual: a person that identifies as the sex they were born as, and are attracted to people of the sex opposite of theirs, who are usually also cis-gendered or cis-sexual. What we used to call people.

WHITE FRAGILITY

White Fragility: Why It's So Hard for White People to Talk About Racism is a 2018 book written by Robin DiAngelo about race relations in the United States. An academic with experience in diversity training, DiAngelo coined the term "white fragility" in 2011 to describe any defensive instincts or reactions that a white person experiences when questioned about race or made to consider their own race. **Wikipedia**

In other words, this is a book, written by a pseudo-academic who earns her living giving race diversity training for large business in the US. It is not scientifically founded in anything other than her desire to earn a living and to have a book to sell at her diversity and inclusion training sessions. In itself, nothing wrong with that. But she has promoted herself as the Queen of "Woke" and has indeed been lauded by the radical left as she defined a term that never before existed, White Fragility, but that makes sense to the guilt ridden, uber rich left-wing politicians and their ignorant minions. It appeals in the main, to rich white people who wish to erase their generations of guilt with an easy catch phrase.

DiAngelo isn't the first person to make a buck pushing tricked-up pseudo-intellectual horseshit as corporate wisdom, but she might be the first to do it selling Hitlerian race theory. White Fragility has a simple message: there is no such thing as a universal human experience, and we are defined not by our individual personalities or moral choices, but only by our racial category.

If your category is "white," bad news: you have no identity apart from your participation in white supremacy ("Anti-blackness is foundational to our very identities... Whiteness has always been predicated on blackness"), which naturally means "a positive white identity is an impossible goal."

This intellectual equivalent of the "ordeal by water" (if you float, you're a witch) is orthodoxy across much of academia.

White Fragility is based upon the idea that human beings are incapable of judging each other by the content of their character, and if people of different races think they are getting along or even loving one another, they probably need immediate antiracism training. This is an important passage because rejection of King's "dream" of racial harmony — not even as a description of the obviously flawed present, but as the aspirational goal of a better future — has become a central tenet of this brand of antiracist doctrine mainstream press outlets are rushing to embrace.

White fragility refers to feelings of discomfort a white person experiences when they witness discussions around racial inequality and injustice.

For example, people of colour may find it difficult to speak to white people about white privilege and superiority. The white person may become defensive, and the person of colour may feel obligated to comfort the white person because we live in a white-dominated environment.

White fragility differs from both white privilege and white supremacy. White privilege refers to the fact that white people have advantages in society that others do not. White supremacy is the belief that people with white skin are superior.

White fragility triggers

Racial stressors may cause a range of defensive behaviours and emotions. White people may act in certain ways when people of colour discuss racism.

Their reactions may include:

- anger
- fear
- guilt
- arguing
- silence
- leaving the stress-inducing situation

By behaving in this way, white people may prevent people of colour from attempting to talk about racism with them.

Different sources of racial stress that white people can experience may come from:

- a person claiming that a white person's views are racist
- a person of colour talking about their racial experiences and perspectives
- a person of colour not protecting a white person's feelings about racism

- a fellow white person not agreeing with another white person's perspectives on racism
- a white person receiving feedback that their behaviour or actions had a racist impact
- a white person being presented with a person of colour in a position of leadership

Other triggers of white fragility may include situations wherein the white race is not central. For example, white fragility may occur when watching a movie where a person of colour is driving the story's action or is in a nonstereotypical role.

History

White fragility is a term that Dr. Robin DiAngelo invented to describe how white people react to issues of racism.

Dr. DiAngelo has a Ph.D. in multicultural education, and her specialty is whiteness studies and critical discourse analysis.

The term came from a paper Dr. DiAngelo wrote in 2011 on race and social injustice, called "White Fragility." The term became popular, and Dr. DiAngelo wrote a book on the topic to further explain how white fragility is promoting racism.

How it differs from racism

Some people may define racism as the belief that a particular race is superior to another. However, others may refer to this as racial prejudice.

Sociologists define racism as an unequal distribution of privileges between white people and people of colour. Racism occurs when white people benefit from an unequal distribution of privileges and people of colour experience deprivation.

For example, one 2019 study Trusted Source examines the various ways in which racism may be impacting healthcare and driving racial inequities in health.

This definition of racism only applies to white people due to white privilege. Historically, white people have not had to experience the same oppression, inequality, and discrimination that people of colour have due to white people holding power.

White people may be against the definition of racism, but experiencing white fragility can contribute to racism. A white person defending themselves or arguing against white superiority prevents conscious discussions with people of colour about race and racism.

Why is it problematic?

People experiencing white fragility may not be racist, but their actions, behaviours, and feelings may promote racism. Avoiding the topic of race contributes to racism. By disregarding the notions of white superiority and white privilege, racism will continue to hold its place in society.

Since white people rarely experience racism, they often cannot see, feel, or understand it. Many people of colour describe having been prepared to live as a minority in a racist society by their parents.

Due to this absence of understanding and experience, white people lack what Dr. DiAngelo calls "racial stamina." However, white people can develop racial stamina by having direct experiences with people of colour and engaging in sometimes difficult conversations with them.

By building racial stamina, white people may be able to manage racial stressors rather than ignoring or silencing them. Conscious and explicit engagement with people of different races can help break the pattern of fragile behaviours and actions related to race.

The sociology behind it

Dr. DiAngelo's research suggests that several factors lead to white fragility in the U.S. These include:

- segregation
- universalism and individualism
- entitlement to racial comfort
- racial arrogance
- racial belonging
- psychic freedom
- white dominance

Most white people live in segregated areas. In these segregated lives, white people receive little information and education about racism. This means that they may be unable to think about racism critically. This can lead to an inability to consider the perspectives of people of colour.

Due to segregated living, white people may perceive a good school or a good neighbourhood as "white." Although discussions about what makes a space good are likely to be racially dependent, white people may deny these ideas.

Another factor in white fragility is the idea that white people are just people, whereas people of colour belong to a race. To them, white people can represent all of humanity, but people of colour may only represent their own races and not humanity in general.

Although white people may be against racism, they may deny that white privilege exists. By objecting to white privilege, white people contradict their objection to racism.

Being in a white-dominant culture is comfortable for a white person. White people may not feel the need to challenge their perspectives about race. By remaining in this comfortable environment, white people try to avoid the topic of racism.

Since white people do not receive teaching to deal with racism in a complex manner, they tend to dismiss more informed perspectives on race rather than acknowledge their lack of understanding.

Although white people may reject racism, they may tend to enjoy a segregated life if people do not label them as racist. In their perspective, if the intention was not to avoid living near people of colour but it happened anyway, it is not segregation. White people may feel racial innocence in such cases.

Also, white people may not understand the social burden of race because they understand that race resides in people of colour. Since white people may not consider themselves part of a race, they are free from carrying the burden of race.

Constant messages in history, media, and advertising — and from our role models, teachers, and everyday conversations about good neighbourhoods and schools — reinforce white fragility. These notions promote the idea that white people are better and more important than people of colour.

Summary

White fragility refers to feelings and behaviours that occur when white people face racial stressors. They may deny white superiority but live a segregated life without any concerns about the absence of people of colour.

Many factors contribute to white fragility, and although it may not be racism, it supports a racist culture. By building racial stamina, however, white people can more openly and critically discuss issues surrounding race.

There is no such thing as white fragility, other than the rather inflammatory title for an appallingly written book.

TOXIC MASCULINITY

From the Urban Dictionary

*A social science term that describes narrow repressive type of ideas about the male gender role, that defines masculinity as exaggerated masculine traits like being violent, unemotional, sexually aggressive, and so forth. Also suggests that men who act too emotional or maybe aren't violent enough or don't do all of the things that "real men" do, can get their "**man card**" taken away.*

*Many people confuse the difference between Masculinity and **toxic Masculinity**. However, one can be masculine without having toxic Masculinity.*

Just in case you haven't read enough unbelievable garbage about these terms and labels, try these:

*Some beliefs (Beliefs? Who says that these are beliefs. The world really is screwed) of **toxic masculinity** is that:*

-interactions between men and women always have to be competitive and not cooperative.

-men can never truly understand women and that men and women can never just be friends.

-That REAL men need to be strong and that showing emotion is a sign of weakness...unless it's anger, that is considered okay.

-The idea that men can never be victims of abuse and talking about it is shameful.

-The idea that REAL men always want sex and are ready for it at any time.

-The idea that violence is the answer to everything and that REAL men solve their problems through violence.

-The idea that men could never be single parents and that men shouldn't be very interactive in their children's learning and development and that men should always be the dominant one in the relationship or else he's a "Cuck."

*-The idea that any interest in a range of things that are strictly considered feminine would be an **emasculation** of a guy.*

THE "CISHET" DILEMMA

"Cishet" or "cis-het," pronounced "SIS-het," is a combination of the "cis" in "cisgender" and the "het" in "heterosexual." It has been used as an adjective and as a noun. It's what we used to call "people".

So what does it mean?

"Cisgender," is an adjective to refer to anyone whose gender identity matches their sex assigned at birth. "Heterosexual," used interchangeably with "straight," has been defined by GLAAD[50] as "An adjective used to describe people whose enduring physical, romantic, and/ or emotional attraction is to people of the opposite sex."

So, at its most basic level, "cishet" is a word to refer to anyone who is straight and cisgender, meaning a person whose gender identity matches

---

[50] https://www.glaad.org/reference/lgbtq

their sex assigned at birth and whose enduring physical, romantic, and emotional attraction is to people of the opposite sex.

Does that mean there are other meanings?

That can depend on a few things: the context of how the word is used, the intent of the person using it, and what meanings the listener might associate with "cishet." In a 2016 blog post for Patheos, Jeana Jorgensen explained "cishet" in a way that went beyond just "straight and cisgender":

When you put cisgender and heterosexual together, you get cis-het: someone whose life experience has been dominated by partaking in two normative identities when it comes to gender identity and sexual orientation. You get someone who's lived their life with those two settings on default mode... which isn't a bad thing, just a thing that means you have a bunch in common with the cultural majority, and that you probably haven't faced oppression for your gender identity or sexuality alone...

...As a descriptor, I think cis-het can be useful shorthand for denoting what someone's life experience has been in these areas. It doesn't tell you much else about them, though, like how their religious views impact their gender and sexuality, or their economic and social class, or ethnicity, and so on.

*Doesn't it just mean, **a person?***

Again, that will depend on the usage. Some will use it in a way to imply cultural and sociological experiences in the way Jorgensen used it above, and others will use it just as a way to say "cisgender and heterosexual" with fewer syllables.

So is it an identity?

Some people will refer to themselves as "cishet" or "cis-het," whereas there are people who will use it to refer to other people, not themselves.

Is it OK to use it to refer to someone else?

Like many terms, there's no agreed-upon rule on it, because different people have different associations with the word. To explain that, we can look at the definitions for it on Urban Dictionary, a site that explains slang terms and colloquial phrases. The user-submitted definitions include "ad hominem attack" and "an insult." Of course, this is not how everyone views the word.

Who thinks of it as an attack or insult?

There are people who are cisgender and heterosexual themselves who find it offensive, as it's a label they themselves would not use for themselves. The common response to that is that if someone *is* both cisgender and heterosexual, calling them "cishet" is not a slur, but just a statement of fact.

So what is the intent?

That will depend, of course. In many message board threads, it seems to be a shorthand to refer to "people who are cisgender and straight" without having to retype "people who are cisgender and straight" over and over again. Many of the people who use it seem cognizant of the word's potential to be misconstrued, as demonstrated by the Reddit thread for the question, "What is a "cishet" and why is it bad?" A person asked, "What is a cishet and why do people want to kill them?" A user responded by saying that the goal is not to harm or antagonize people who are cisgender and heterosexual, but rather get them to appreciate what life must be like for other people who are not cisgender and/or not transgender:

In some circles, however, there is a certain animosity present towards "cishets" because the world is ruled by cishets. Cishets are the ones who created, are acknowledged in, and are protected by our laws, social norms, and media, while the existence of non-cishet people is largely ignored (and in particular, non-white-cishet people, at least in the US). But only a very few fringe activists actually believe that cishet people should die. Most just want them to recognize their privilege and work to make life better for those without privilege, or at least not actively make their lives worse.

In her blog post, Jorgensen made a similar point when explaining why some LGBTQ+ people want to have their own spaces:

There are times when I'm sick of educating on a Feminism 101 level and really want to dig into the deep stuff with my peers who already "get it." Since so much of mainstream culture is already dominated by the viewpoints of, and comfortable for, cis-het folks, it makes sense to carve out alternative spaces where cis-het people either have to take a back seat and listen to the experiences of others, or be excluded entirely (I think there should still be some events where they're welcome, in the spirit of building an inclusive sex-positive movement, though). I don't believe that people should be put down on account of their gender identity or sexual orientation, so using cis-het as a slur doesn't sit well with me. At the same time, I understand feeling like they've dominated so much social space, thus wanting to have your own space free of their voices.

So when people get defensive about the word, are they getting defensive about the word, or the context in which it is used?

That is a good question. The words "cisgender" and "heterosexual" appear in so many contexts that it's hard to associate any one set of emotions or feelings with the words. They appear in news stories and all sorts of other contexts where they are used as neutral descriptor terms, so there's no one connotation for each of those words. People who see the word "cishet" or "cis-het," on the other hand, might only see that word in the context of people calling out the privileges that they feel cisgender and heterosexual people have. If they only see the word in the context of serious discussions about serious topics, then "cishet" might not seem normalized for them as a basic descriptor that only means "cisgender" and "heterosexual." Instead, they might see the word as loaded with specific feelings and connotations. As one Reddit user explained:

It shouldn't be used as an insult, you're right. At the same time, if it comes across as an insult, it's probably because the cishet isn't being agreed with and someone pointed out that they are CisHet and don't actually have any idea what they are talking about in this hypothetical situation. People don't respond well to being told "hey, you're wrong... like... completely" while hearing a term they've never considered before.

Similarly, a user on a Susan's Place message board said this about labels:

I think if more people used these terms in everyday language, rather than using them to express bitterness, they would become more accepted by the general public. No cis person identifies as "cis," though. It's just a term we use because it's easier than saying "non-trans non-intersex." People don't like being labelled by other people, even if there is no bitterness attached.

So, how do I know when to use it? How can I use it in a way that's as a descriptor, not as a slur?

There's no agreed-upon rule, and in her blog post, Jorgensen said even she struggles with that question:

What's the line between wanting a space for folks who aren't cis-het to be truly front and centre for once, and being outright discriminatory against cis-het folks? ...Words are useful to describe our experiences, but also risk being over-generalizations. I think "cis-het" has its useful moments, but I'm wary of its potential to be used against people...

On most LGBTQ+ Experiment posts, the rule of thumb is that it's safest not to apply a word to someone if they wouldn't use that word as a self-descriptor. In the case of "cishet" or "cis-het," many people would think it's just a statement of fact, condensing the neutral truths that a person is both "cisgender" and "heterosexual." "Cishet" is not a commonly used word outside of online forums, so be prepared to explain it when using it, just in case the term is not understood by everyone. And be prepared for the fact that some folks might push back against it.

INTERSECTIONALITY

Intersectionality is an analytical framework for understanding how aspects of a person's social and political identities combine to create different modes of discrimination and privilege. The term was conceptualized and coined by Kimberlé Williams Crenshaw in 1989.

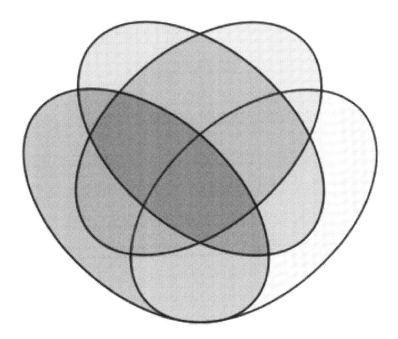

But how on earth can this constitute a label for some gender dysphoric, CisHet, white male, father, parent, husband, friend. That is nonsense. Intersectional has been added to pride of place on the alphabet soup that is: LGBTQIAAP+ or whatever that might be this week.

THE WOKE PROPHET

"I was the only child of two barristers. I learnt early on that my private education and frequent family holidays to Montenegro and the Maldives were merely a ruse by which my parents could distract me from my oppression."

Titania McGrath (McGrath)

Karl Marx's ultimate achievement (or failure) seems to be the Russian Revolution of 1917, it is perhaps timely to ponder 104 years later about Marxism's current relevance.

Understandably, this exercise will be seen by many as a waste of time. The fall of the Soviet Union and the subsequent dismantling of communism as a world political force appear to be events strong enough to have sent Marxism to Trotsky's proverbial dustbin of history. From this perspective, it is not surprising how quickly the whole amalgam of Marxist theory dealing with doctrine and praxis, that was printed, diffused, taught and discussed in Western academic and political circles, evaporated in the early 1990s. Marxist theory fundamentally lost appeal because it was intimately associated with a vast political failure.

148

Yet, there are two current world events, as important as the fall of the Soviet Union, that also need to be considered in this analysis. First, the growing inability of capitalism, particularly its American distilled version, to answer the social and economic aspirations of extensive sectors of the population in North America and Europe, as demonstrated by the aftermath of the Great Recession of 2008. More compelling, the economy with the leading edge in the world (China) follows an economic model (socialism) fundamentally different from conventional capitalism and, to add insult to injury, still maintains within its theoretical framework a reverence (albeit discreet) for Marx's thought.

If the debate on Marxism's relevance is therefore worth considering, we should briefly examine what Marxism is all about.

Only traditional political opponents to Marxism assign to it a uniformity that it never had. Marxists, on the other hand, used to collide in distinguishing and dissecting Marxism in abstract and in the context of political tactics and strategy. For instance, some emphasized the thoughts of the young pre-1848 Marx (particularly on alienation), whereas others would only consider the socio-economic analysis that culminated in *Capital*. Others were dazzled primarily by Marx's philosophical thought and built theoretical schools around dialectic materialism. More significantly, differing social analysis and political action led to numerous breakdowns around the confrontation between reformist social democracy and revolutionary Marxism.

It can also be argued that classical Marxism was buried in the early days of the Russian Revolution. The Soviet upheaval meant political events that did not coincide at all with Marx's predictions: a social earthquake in a poor and backward country (not in a wealthy, advanced western industrialized society as he had prophesized) and a revolution that for several decades, contrary to Marx's predictions, did not become a world event. Additionally, the tactical alliance between workers and peasants, a fundamental scheme of the Russian Revolution, did not enter into Marx's political or theoretical play the way it was schemed by the Bolshevik leaders or in early Communist China.

Timing explains to a great extent the gap between Marx's predictions, the political events that he inspired in Russia, and the aftermath of the October Revolution. The Russian Revolution took place 50 years after the first publication of *Capital*. While the economic environment described by Marx was still predominant at the time of the Revolution, that has not been the case during the last 50 years. Marx's economic analysis was focused on a world dominated by manufacturing. Marx did not (or could not) see the potential value added from trade related activities. This of course is more evident today as services play a growing economic role through international trade and world finance. As our globe is different from Marx's, it is difficult to assign *predictive* power to Marxism as it claimed to have 100 years ago.

As an *interpretation* instrument, however, Marxism seems to be a different matter. At the root of Marx's thoughts was the belief that economic conditions play a significant role in social evolution and, therefore, there is a need to understand these conditions not only for analytical purposes but also as a basis of political action.

From this perspective, events such as the ongoing and growing dislocation of the American political system or the increasing political resistance to globalization efforts through projects such as the European Union are easier to understand. Growing world unemployment (in some European countries currently at levels similar to the ones during the Great Recession of 1929), the perceived divorce between power elites and people's aspirations, and the widening wealth gap can help grasp the roots of these political conflicts.

Beyond its potential interpretation value, it is also worth considering if Marxism still has a role as a *functioning political tool*. To assess this, we need to consider one of the classical controversies around Marx's thought, that is his views on human nature. Marxists believed that material conditions explain to a great extent failure on social progress. This belief was criticized for denying or at least minimizing the value of political action, i.e. human will. Although this controversy never subsumed and has been used numerous times by Marx's detractors, political action was never denied by Marx and he himself was a major political player, for instance at the time of the Paris Commune and as founder of the First International.

To assess the value of Marxism as political praxis, we need to remember that a political device, to be effective, does not need to have a scientifically proven theory behind it. A good example is religion, the most unscientific belief, as basis for political action. Although Marx dismissed the value of religion, he was well aware of the role it played in social change during the European religious wars. Faith in a better world or in the afterlife not only moves mountains, but also topples governments and changes societies.

Growing awareness of the socio-economic failures of today's western social architecture gives validity to Marxism as a potential political tool. As long as people believe that there is unfairness and exploitation, right or wrong, Marxism will have a role to play as a theory capable of justifying political action. Even if Marxism is perceived as a failure as a result of the demise of the Soviet Union and its Eastern European satellites, or even if Marxism is dismissed as lacking economic or scientific soundness, its political and interpretative value, including everything that we know as the extreme failures of Marxism, still seem relevant to advocates of woke ideology today.

Karl Mark – No attribution available

I wonder, dear reader, if Karl Marx could see us today in our modern world, if he would be proud of his legacy of if he would be laughing at as. I suspect that his capitalistic side, given that he spent his rather hedonistic life borrowing money from others and in considerable debt, would also come out and he would just think it was a jolly good laugh. After all Marxism is great...if your rich!

Socialism is the principle that everyone deserves to be equal, even the poor. Critics point to the fact that socialist governments in the past have failed to eliminate poverty. But this is a misunderstanding of our aims. If there were no poor people, then there would be no point in socialism, which would make us all capitalists by default. And why would anyone want that?

McGrath, Titania. Woke: A Guide to Social Justice (p. 53). Little, Brown Book Group. Kindle Edition.

THE MODERN LEFT AND FASCISM

Fascist movements are implicitly utopian because they—like communist and heretical Christian movements—assume that with just the right arrangement of policies, all contradictions can be rectified. This is a political siren song; life can never be made perfect, because man is imperfect. (Goldberg 130)

Far too often socialism and communism are compared to what is currently the political embodiment of the modern leftist ideology in the U.S. These leftist and communist ideas include anti-capitalism, total destruction of the individual in favour of the state, and big government takeover. We have all heard this stereotype.

However, I think there is a far more accurate political ideology floating in the minds of modern leftists, thirsty for revolution to take down "the man" and *change* the "bourgeois system." I am speaking of fascism.

"What!!" you say as you spit out your soy latte.

"Fascism is reserved only for evil white conservative men who spout evil fascist rhetoric like small government, individualism, self-reliance, capitalism, less dependency on government, traditionalism, and self-responsibility with strong ties to self-sustaining autonomous Christian family units!!!"

Slow down, Che, put down the vegan burger and let me explain…

After peeling back some layers and layers of Orwellian leftist language and indoctrination that fascism is of the evil American Right, closer examination reveals startling comparisons to the modern American leftist. Fascism could not be any further from the American conservative (Classical Liberalism at its heart). Very few realize that fascism by its very nature was an extremely leftist populist movement taking root in Mussolini's Italy and spreading like wild fire throughout Europe.

Fascism was born out of socialism (the prized ideology among the left) and was an evolved state-centric version of socialism which became popular around the early to mid 1900s. It was "new" and full of revolutionary change. Benito Amilcare Andrea Mussolini (a name consisting almost entirely of Socialist revolutionaries) was raised a charismatic Italian Socialist (his Socialist father being a huge influence on him) (Goldberg 31).

After Mussolini incorporated socialism and nationalism within Italy, fascism spread quickly (without much pretence to race that would come later with German Nazism). Fascism would eventually compete with International Socialism for the young revolutionary, the working man, the poor, and the masses in places such as Germany, France, and Italy.

To many individuals, fascism state-centric ideology seemed far more of a "working system" rather than that delusional idea of "uniting the workers of the world", which was the motto of the International Socialist. With fascism, as with all large bloated governments that leftists think can cure all our qualms, the utopian lie is propagated by the state which supposedly aims to build a communal National Socialism state-sponsored family.

Fascism was to transcend class differences exactly like socialism preached. Below are first-hand accounts according to working class Germans and their views on Hitler's Nationalist Socialist ideas.

Below are key points from Mussolini and the Fasci di Combattimento (a Fascist organization created by Mussolini) circa 1919 (Goldberg 46):

- *The abolition of the senate and the creation of a national technical council on intellectual and manual labour, industry, commerce and culture*
- *The creation of various government bodies run by worker's representatives*
- *The obligation of the state to build "rigidly secular" schools for the raising of "the proletariat's moral and cultural condition"*

All of this seems like the modern American leftist's wet dream. Modern American leftist rhetoric is far closer to fascism than the American right's strong stress on individualism, capitalism, and reduced government intervention.

Fascism stressed huge state governments. This huge fascist government included expanding health services, enforcing anti-elitism, wealth-confiscation, and secularism (Goldberg 46) all in the name of the state and the common good. Fascism offered "anti-bourgeois, anti-capitalistic, and anti-individualist nationalism" (Sternhell 214-220).

The state was always before the individual under fascism; taking from some and redistributing to the many. This is the core of modern American leftist ideology. Many parallels of fascism are closely similar to Obamacare (expanding health services), higher taxes among the elite and wealthy (wealth confiscation), and the most recent; the fascist power grab, by the FCC "Net Neutrality" rules (anti-capitalist).

To illustrate this comparison further, let's look at just a few of the Nazi Party's key points (Goldberg 411):

- We demand the nationalization of all (previous) associated industries (trusts).
- We demand a division of profits of all heavy industries.
- The first obligation of every citizen must be to work both spiritually and physically. The activity of individuals is not to counteract the interests of the universality, but must have its result within the framework of the whole for the benefit of all.

I can't tell the difference when the Nazi points end and the American leftist points begin. Not to mention, affirmative action (prized among the left) is just race privilege enforced by government intervention. Affirmative action is similar to the notorious government enforced Aryan privilege in Nazi Germany regardless of skill.

In all leftist extremes, be it communism, Nazism, socialism, or Fascism; murder, violence, and censorship are sure to be the eventual outcome of huge government. It is a historic pattern and if history is cyclical, which I believe it is, we are at the beginning of what will be the eventual violence found among extreme Leftist purity tactics dating back to the French Revolution (Jacboins), up through Soviet Russia (Bolsheviks), Ukraine, and Communist China.

Nothing has been more devastating and dangerous politically in the 20th century than leftist thought. If we look at 20th century communism alone we come to a whopping 85-100 million worldwide that perished under such leftist regimes, not to mention the censorship, labour camps, violation of civil liberties, and imprisonment.

One should think of fascism not as the complete opposite of socialism and communism, but yet another kindred spirit in extreme leftist political ideologies that were competing for the hearts and minds of the populous. Not much has changed with fascist ideology of collectivism (another prized belief of the left) were individual twigs bundle together to make a strong piece of collective wood.

Allow this article to be a possible warning sign of modern day ideology, as their quest will devolve into a loss of civility and violence as we move farther and farther left. As the left ideologies become more and more resembling a preacher preaching piety from the pulpit, "action" will be the next conclusive step. Peel back the leftist Orwellian language with nice sounding words like "Obamacare" and "Net Neutrality" to expose it for what it really is; fascist policies and huge government takeover in a pretty wrapper.

Whatever the case, one should keep in mind that socialism, communism, fascism, and Nazism all are of the left; they were just different factions of the left. What is occurring in the U.S. today is not that different from what occurred in Europe some years ago. Though it may be much slower and softer, "American" Fascism echoes European Fascism and is rooted in this very ideology.

Keep this in mind when you are sitting in your cubc at the Ministry of Truth, hunched over your keyboard, editing and bowdlerizing Wikipedia pages for "the party"; just remember this article and the quintessential fascist party ideology:

"But it was all right, everything was all right, the struggle was finished. He had won the victory over himself. He loved Big Brother."

Do not become the protagonist of 1984. Let's keep fiction for the books and reality for us here in America. The philosophical and political fate of the country depends on it.

Works Cited:

Goldberg, Jonah "Liberal Fascism" (New York: Doubleday, 2007)

Sternhell, Zeev "Neither Right or Left: Fascist Ideology in France." (Princeton, New Jersey: Princeton University Press, 1995)

THE DEATH OF THE SO-CIAL CONTRACT

Society can't exist without some sort of contractual obligation between citizen and government and worryingly there are warnings that ours is dying. Jean-Jacques Rousseau's best-known quote from his 1762 thesis On the Social Contract, (see appendix I) suggests that "Man is born free; but everywhere he is in chains." Rousseau was concerned with how governments form uneasy alliances with their citizens; how they wield power; and maintain a cosy relationship with the world of commerce. Despite what many global politicians think, ideas do have the power to get people protesting, even storming the Bastille and assembling guillotines. Recently, the citizens of France where caught up in a May Day protest on Paris's Place de République, I watched, dumb stuck, as on the TV the flares began, and the dogs and their heavily armed minders appeared. Here, I guessed, was a people not used, or willing, to be pushed around. The French are still quite good at that…standing up for their rights. Perhaps we should all be a little better at it.

In fact, the French education ministry has issued a ruling that bans the use of gender-neutral language in public schools claiming the "woke" push was a danger to the country and a threat to the French language, as the Daily Wire reports:

"The country's education ministry issued the ruling last week after a push to include full stops in the middle of written words – dubbed 'midpoints' – which allow both male and female forms to be represented simultaneously," The Daily Mail reported. "In French grammar, nouns take on the gender of the subject to which they refer, with male preferred over female in mixed settings."

"The Académie Française, a nearly 400-year-old institution that guards the French language, pushed back on the attempt to make the

language woke, saying that it is "harmful to the practice and under-standing of [French.]"

"Nathalie Elimas, the State Secretary for Priority Education, said on Thursday that the attempts to make the language woke were "a danger for our country" and "the death knell for the use of French in the world."

"Elimas said that the move would not make the language more popular and instead would drive people to learn English instead. With the spread of inclusive writing, the English language – already quasi-heg-emonic across the world – would certainly and perhaps forever defeat the French language," she said."

It's a sad day when France takes a stand about the danger the "wokeists" on the left represent that more political leaders in the USA should have taken long ago. The use of gender neutral and "woke" language is a threat not only to the French language but also to the very fabric and core of our society and culture. The woke left claims to be "inclusive" and "tolerant" but the truth is they are anything but inclusive and toler-ant. Leftists, especially those involved with public education want to extinguish any views they deem "harmful" and teach our children that the USA is an evil and racist place. The "wokeists" are very clearly an existential threat to our way of life and their policies and ideas need to be fought at every turn.

But I digress, back to Rousseau.

Rousseau made it clear that "laws are always useful to those with possessions and harmful to those who have nothing". Such was the case in France under the reign of Louis XV the (not so) Beloved. Economic inequality; lack of opportunities for people to realise their potential, sleep in a house, eat anything but cake. As Louis's grandson found out, a society can't exist without some sort of contractual obligation between citizen and government. A contract fiercely protected in France, still, curated in other Western countries, especially after national emergencies (England's National Health Service established in July 1948). And across western governments, the great egalitarian experiment that gave us everything from school milk to Welfare. But now there are signs that our own social contract is weakening and in some cases dying. Small clues, accumulating so slowly we barely notice: a proliferation of taxes, from wine equalisation to stamp duty; increased waiting times for elective surgery; the spread of outer suburbs that provide an endless flow of stamp duty; and conversely, a drop of between 5 and 30 per cent in national rates of volunteering between 2014 and 2018, the daily news ringing with the same tales of dysfunction around the globe.

Australia, 2018, and the New South Wales Corrections Minister, David Elliott, explains that the new Clarence Correctional Centre will have an "open campus-style design" with such joys as tablets that "enable them to complete vocational educational training". No copies of Rousseau in this new 1700- bed facility, built on the equivalent of 180 football fields. Rehabilitation, of course, is admirable, but the images of pre-fabricated cells, and kilometres of wire, make me wonder if this isn't some sort of growth industry. Or at least, that our governments are expecting more customers in the coming years. Why? Rousseau, again, explaining that the social contract is a delicate beast. "As soon as any man says of the affairs of the State, 'What does it matter to me?' the State may be given up for lost." I ask myself what this means to the extra 1,000,000 (generally not-so-well-off and predominantly Black) United States citizens the state governments expect to welcome to the corrections system in the next three years.

I know you're thinking, here we go, Lenin's on his soapbox. Perhaps socialism is just another form of illegitimacy. Just the same, political power is a slippery eel. Like Barack Obama, in August 2012, explaining how a "red line for us is we start seeing a whole bunch of chemical weapons moving around or being utilised", becoming, a few days later, a watered-down statement about Assad's obligations and accountability. Nothing, compared to Donald Trump's decision (according to Jackson Diehl) "to excuse Saudi Arabia's Mohammed bin Salman for ordering the murder and dismemberment of one of his own citizens". Ignoring the CIA, and common sense, Trump makes truth a strangely distant and unimportant concern so that "we shouldn't be surprised if more exiled dissidents disappear or die". No mention of oil prices, or the $110 billion in arms Riyadh has promised to purchase from the US this year alone (2021).

So what's going on with the social contract? Is there a connection between leaders like Donald Trump, and the educational outcomes of poor kids? Between the millions of different taxes citizens of the world pay, and the diminishing level of services we all receive? What even is the

163

social contact anymore? Do people matter, or are we becoming liabilities to the state?

In my home nation of Australia, the state governments would seem to be free to establish various schemes of taxation as they see fit. Here is how it works; get the Lotteries Commission to find an operator and allow them to set up gaming tables and poker machines. Then we keep 13.75 per cent of gaming revenue, licence fees and (as a Christmas bonus) unclaimed prizes. This stuff is genius.

Repeated, at a national scale, so that in 2015 Australian governments were earning $5.8 billion a year from gambling. Problem gamblers, broken families, suicides, all apparently made legitimate by government warnings to curb your gambling.

Somehow, in our brave new world of endless choice and individual (by name only) freedoms, any fallout is your own problem. I mean, you could've chosen not to, couldn't you? What would Rousseau make of the misery that comes from the Australian experiment in gambling? Would he be surprised that $23 billion dollars annually is spent on gambling. Not books, shoes, school fees, shopping, medicines? Australia as a giant Monaco, or Macau, slowly giving up any sense of a fair go as handshakes are made, promises whispered and politicians paid off.

Don't for one minute think that this is only in Australia. It is the system I know best and, at the same time, ashamed of.

The late cultural theorist, Mark Fisher[51], described a corporate-political lovefest that aims to "keep us in a state of panicked anxiety … and radical competitive individualism so that we can't act together and gain a collective agency". Instead, functioning individually, wired into a world where technology will save us, connect us to a community of the like-minded, encourage our creativity and sense of self-worth. But what we're really left with is a semi-medicated existence where, all of a sudden, and for no reason, we feel like crying. A world that breeds loneliness and isolation, only ever giving the impression of satisfaction. Homes where we need Siri to remind us to shit; where our babies are wired into tablets before their parents. Where students sit in front of laptops for hours on end, edu-managerialists claiming this approach (generally maths-focussed – Western civilisation seems to have less potential for profit) to learning might lead to faster computation, better memory, understanding of high-level scientific concepts. Might make better technocrats, entrepreneurs, to build faster machines to replace more people who can sit around strung out on drugs or anti-depressants, or just make their way straight to the Clarence Correctional Centre.

---

[51] Born in 1968, Mark was part of a prominent generation of British thinkers who grew up in and were formed by the vibrant culture of post-war Britain. Author of *Capitalist Realism* he sadly passed away on January 13th 2017 at the age of 48.

POLITICS NO LONGER SERVES ANY PRACTICAL PURPOSE

More than 700 million people - or 10 per cent of the global population - still live in extreme poverty, which means they are surviving on less than $1.90 a day. Experts predict these figures will continue to rise as a result of the COVID-19 crisis alongside the ongoing impacts of conflicts and climate change. Improving the lives of the poorest and most vulnerable; ensuring no one is left behind is an overarching theme of the Sustainable Development Goals (SDGs) and the primary focus of Goal 1: No Poverty. In order to achieve the vision set out in the SDGs, the fundamental issue of poverty must be addressed.

Poverty is about more than a lack of income. It has a range of different socioeconomic dimensions, including: the ability to access services and social protection measures and to express opinions and choice; the power to negotiate; and social status, decent work and opportunities. Poverty is also the root cause of many human rights and labour rights violations. For example, child labour, forced labour and human trafficking are each deeply connected to poverty.

Just what exactly are our politicians contributing to any of the above issues. I have experienced the evidence of the death of our Social Contract here in rich Norway. Yes, apparently one of the richest countries on earth, where school teachers are employed by the school headmaster and there is no requirement for any qualifications what so ever. No possibility of corruption there then.

Norway claims universal health care…by redefining "universal". The much-misunderstood myth is that Healthcare in Norway is free…well…sort of true but only after you pay the egenandel – deductible. Which can be anything from 210NOK (c.$21USD) to many thousands of Kroner depending on the service. Your doctor or fastlege (GP), is effectively appointed to you by the state. You are free to change your fastlegen up to 4 times a year…if you can find one with a vacancy. Yes, even in Norway there is corruption, dishonesty and legal perils. In fact one of the wonders of the Norwegian legal system is that if the crime you have been accused of, carries a sentence of less than 6 months in prison, you are not entitled to appear with a lawyer. The case is not heard and argued at all. It is arbitrarily decided by a Judge who meters out fines that can be as high as your annual salary as he or she sees fit. And guess what qualifications the Norwegian legal system requires for its junior judges? And this is in Norway, the most corrupt country in Scandinavia.

WHAT SOCIAL CONTRACT?

Another face of the ailing social contract. Propaganda in place of debate; the appearance of democratic process, although, as anyone who's ever protested a local, state or federal government decision knows, it's never about the will of the majority. If a roof's blown off in a storm, a politician is required to appear in front of the house, say something like,

"There are no free kicks in this country, you just gotta pick yerself up and get back on the field," before returning to his or her car and pissing off. Everything is our problem, our fault; for not watching the speedo when we reach the bottom of the hill; not having enough money to send our kids to a private school; not having health insurance; for using too much electricity, water or gas. The wheels turn and our governments, sure we can be pacified that little bit more, build another stadium/hotel combo, print more brochures and employ more media advisors.

Solution? We, citizens of the world, need to start taking our politicians to account; to challenge their media releases, to question their (apparent) logic. We need, sometimes, to stop doing things how and when we're told to, to protest, actively, like the nothing-to-lose mob on the Place de République. At stake, as it always has been, is the social contract. Rousseau reminded us that "absolute silence … is the image of death". It seems that in a world of constant noise, opinions, Twitter and Facebook, nothing is actually discussed, planned beyond the next election, or questioned.

And I for one, don't remember being asked to sign the damn contract in the first place.

WHITE PEOPLE SHOULD STOP USING THE TERM 'WOKE"

Getty Images

On April 19th, 2021. Dana Brownlee, who titles herself as a 50-year-old Black woman, keynote speaker/trainer and workplace antiracism thought leader, published a thoughtful and thought-provoking article on-line referring to the idea that; White People must stop using the word woke. The article starts with the following rather clear and strong paragraph;

"I have to confess that for years every time I heard the term "race card" interjected into a conversation, it felt like nails on a chalkboard. Immediately, the hairs stood up on the back of my neck, and my amygdala warned me that the person I was engaging with was both insensitive and dangerous. Now, our society is arguably in the midst of a racial reckoning nearly a year after George Floyd's murder, and the public relations winds have radically shifted. Companies and individuals who previously eschewed (if not demonized) racial justice platforms/protests like Black Lives Matter and Colin Kaepernick have instead raced to affirm their support and solidarity with anti-racism related hashtags, social media posts and donations. No, we don't hear the phrase "race card" mentioned much in daily conversation any longer, but a new term, just as insidious, has cropped up to take its place - woke."

She goes on the discuss that Woke is problematic for two primary reasons. First, it's an offensive cultural appropriation. As is disturbingly often the case, White people (or any racial group outside the term's origin) will sometimes begin using a term that originated in a community of colour often as a term of pride, endearment, or self-empowerment years or decades later while either wilfully or inadvertently distorting the original meaning of the term. While any significant analysis of what cultural appropriation is and why it's problematic is considered "beyond the scope of the article", but no word on why that is the case. Suffice it to say that Ms Brownlee claims, that upon hearing White people randomly label individuals and organizations as "woke", she finds this often an unsettling, if not infuriating experience.

170

She writes; "*I first heard the term "stay woke" within the Black community more than a decade ago to mean "stay vigilant", "don't be fooled", or "don't sleep" (to revive an even older relic of colloquial Black parlance). Soon, the term "woke" found its way into broader society to connote someone who is racially conscious. While this version is still intended to connote a positive quality, its use is arguably still problematic.*"

Again, I am missing context for this claim and do not quite follow as to why this would be considered problematic. But I accept that the appropriation of terms, expressions and words from their original usage may seem problematic, as is the case with all common language, but it surely is only the case if the original intent and meaning are lost or subverted. Sadly, as vernacular grows in use, often the original intent does get clouded in usage and the original intent is superseded by a new "accepted" usage.

"Woke" is an example of good intentions leading us to hell," explains Michael Bach, diversity expert and author of the best-selling book *Birds of All Feathers: Doing Diversity and Inclusion Right.* "People who say they're woke, are never woke." Dr. Kathy Obear, President, Centre for Transformation and Change questions, "Is proclaiming 'I'm woke' just the latest variation of how we white people try to dodge scrutiny and critique by saying, 'I'm a good one! My best friend is Black!'"

However, in more recent months, the term has increasingly traded it's more positive-intentioned "conscious" connotation for a pejorative, condescending one. Increasingly, influencers (oftentimes but not always White) have latched onto the term "woke" and weaponized it as an easy way to dismiss or discount a racial issue, platform or grievance offhand as extreme or utterly nonsensical. To be fair, are there issues, platforms, or grievances on the topic of race that are extreme and utterly nonsensical? Certainly, as that would be true of any topic, but this deceptively simple four-letter word has become the anti-racism napalm that we don't need in the struggle for heightened awareness and sensitivity around complex racial issues.

Second, the term's use often prevents the deep, honest, sometimes uncomfortable conversation that arguably is our only pathway to real reconciliation. Let's face it – engaging in sensitive, nuanced conversations around race is challenging enough without the irresponsible insertion of the term "woke" providing an ideological off ramp that shuts down any real listening, learning or self-reflection on issues that really require all three for authentic progress. "Throwing terms like 'woke' around as a way to dismiss the very real and consequential concerns of an entire group of people is just another way of saying, 'I don't want to be inconvenienced by your pain,'" insists equity consultant and C-suite advisor, Tara Jaye Frank. In fact, when White people weaponize the term "woke" during a discussion, it doesn't just disrespectfully discount that specific person or issue but also sends a not-so-subtle message to their peers that if something *feels* extreme to you, you have license to just discount it. This type of signalling is counterproductive if not dangerous.

Brownlee claims; *"After all, White people prioritizing their feelings over racial justice progress is arguably what has held us in a purgatory of racial inequity for centuries."*

I consider Brownlee to be an articulate communicator and I'm sure her Equity and Diversity training is of considerable value, and certainly more intelligent than the nonsense training offered by Diangelo[52] (ibid), but I cannot ignore the use of the word "inequity" in the above quote rather than "inequality".

Widely considered a White liberal thought leader, Bill Maher frequently weaponizes the term "woke" to discount, ridicule or otherwise belittle an issue or idea related to race on his HBO show *Real Time with Bill Maher*. While Maher continues to acknowledge the scourge of racism and has arguably raised and supported issues of racial equality and justice over the years, during this particular season of heighted racial sensitivity and curiosity, he perplexingly seems to have doubled down on a convenient, self-affirming formula of selecting a fringe, outlier or otherwise provocative or misunderstood race related issue, then playing a game of ideological hacky sack with a group of often all-White commentators (with no particular expertise in anti-racism). Yes, it's easy to toss up a broad slogan like "Defund the police" and spend the next several minutes taking turns swiping critiques, but it would be so much more instructive to engage a racial justice expert to help move the discussion beyond the slogan. As noted in this Brookings Institute article,

---

[52] See White Fragility

173

they'd possibly explain that "defunding the police" doesn't imply abolishing policing but instead "means reallocating or redirecting funding away from the police department to other government agencies funded by the local municipality." As many localities grapple with the realities of police forces that are arguably overburdened, undertrained and yes, often tragically influenced by racial bias, it's more than reasonable to begin reimagining what policing looks like going forward. For many localities, this might involve reducing the scope of the traditional policing model, standing up "quality of life" or social service programs or patrols to help address non-violent incidents or mental health concerns, and yes, possibly redirecting some funds to support said programs. But, instead of having that thoughtful discussion, the idea is labelled "woke," then ridiculed and disposed of.

During Maher's recent Sharon Osbourne interview after her highly-publicized departure from *The Talk*, there was a conspicuous omission of any specific discussion of her reported on-air outburst (for which she later apologized) which in concert with subsequent race related allegations prompted CBS to place *The Talk* on hiatus. Instead, their discussion focused on fault they found with others. Osbourne called out Prince Harry as the poster boy for White privilege. She declared herself to be "angry and hurt" by the recent events, expressed frustration with the difficulty of knowing what is "correct and woke for your language that day," and referenced former colleagues as "disgruntled ladies" while Maher blatantly stated that his view was that "nothing happened" during the incident. He later rejected the concept of either of them re-educating themselves on the topic of race. He insisted that because Osbourne has "travelled the world, is married to a rock star and has been with the A-listers," she couldn't possibly need re-education. The goal of the "interview" seemed much more focused on painting Osbourne as a victim than exploring or considering any range of perspectives or underlying racial considerations. In contrast, MSNBC host Tiffany Cross' response to race related dustups involving the likes of Meghan McCain and Sharon Osbourne; whether you agree with her perspective or not, illuminates the fact that as these high-profile incidents surface, there really are deep underlying issues and varying perspectives to consider, and dismissing them as woke extremism is more than a missed opportunity.

Any student of the American civil rights struggle should be well acquainted with the White liberal's history of complicated and capricious commitment to true anti-racism progress. Arguably, this current boomerang effect of sorts may be the result of White progressives deeming themselves to be "woke" (in the sense of being racially conscious and progressive) and therefore in a position to become the arbiter of what is "too much" on the road to racial equity. "The act of 'being woke' is racial arrogance/ignorance, at best, or intentional White supremacy, at worst," insists anti-racist leadership consultant, Tracey Benson, Ed. L.D. "The woke White is and has always been the most dangerous racist in our society, because they outnumber self-realized racists at least 100-1, and furthermore because they have absolved themselves from complicity in White supremacy, shielded themselves from criticism and further learning (especially from people of colour) while simultaneously contributing to and benefitting from societal racism." Indeed, as Dr. Martin Luther King, Jr. noted in his famous letter from a Birmingham jail, "I must confess that over the last few years I have been gravely disappointed with the White moderate. I have almost reached the regrettable conclusion that the Negro's great stumbling block in the stride toward freedom is not the White Citizens Councillor or the Ku Klux Klanner but the White moderate who is more devoted to order than justice; who prefers a negative peace which is the absence of tension to a positive peace which is the presence of justice; who constantly says, 'I agree with you in the goal you seek, but I can't agree with your methods of direct action'; who paternalistically feels that he can set the timetable for another man's freedom; who lives by the myth of time; and who constantly advises the Negro to wait until a 'more convenient season.'" While there's very little to be certain of in this moment of racial reckoning, I'm certain that real progress will require more listening, not less, an inclination towards learning, not a stubborn resistance to new ideas, more opening up, less shutting down, more introspection, less defensiveness, more facts and truth, less visceral dismissiveness, more grace and respect and less self-righteous indignation. Using the term "woke" to stigmatize someone else's perspective is immature and offensive. It feels dehumanizing…just like "the race card" because after all, for many of us racism isn't a game.

The fact that any particular ideology, policy or idea can go too far or lose the benefit-cost ratio battle should go without saying, and it's preposterous to even entertain the suggestion that simply because a person of colour suggests or promotes an idea or platform, it should automatically be adopted (again, beyond obvious). So, when you find yourself in disagreement with an idea, platform or policy related to race, just say so. If the issue is that flawed, it should be easy enough to pick it apart on the merits, right? Everyone is entitled to their opinion and offering a different perspective, asking questions, analysing pros and cons all show a basic level of respect for all parties involved, but labelling something as "woke" as a means of arrogantly dismissing it often feels like a convenient cop out for those who seem allergic to self-reflection, thoughtful analysis....or maybe accountability.

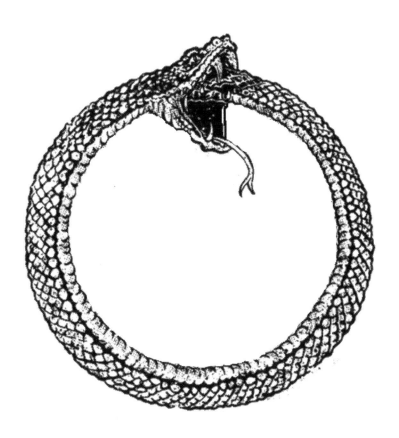

The Ouroboros is an ancient symbol depicting a serpent or dragon eating its own tail. The concept of a creature consuming itself has been interpreted to mean many things over the centuries. Fundamentally, and at one level, it is an Alchemic symbol of self-destruction however it can have a multitude of meanings from destruction to re-birth.

"Intersectionality is a dragon that will eat its own tail"
Jordan B. Peterson

PART 4: OUROBOROS

The Wokeists are eating their own.

As it was with the French Revolution and Robespierre, Napoleon, Hitler, Mussolini, Chavez, Castro, Stalin, Lenin, Mao, Gadhafi and many more; The ultimate victims of these Marxist systems are the Marxists themselves. Eventually, revolutions tend to consume themselves. Just like the ancient symbol of the Ouroboros; these social diseases start by eating the tail. People that the revolution casts as its enemies. White people, Men, Republicans, Conservatives, Classical Musicians, independent thinkers, the Police, Female Sports, Biological Science, and common sense are all struck down, devoured and excommunicated from Social Media, Main Stream Media, Universities and schools. Careers are destroyed and good people are shamed. Whether it's by cancel culture or by lunatic demonstrations on University campuses declaring all white people as oppressors and the enemy. All over the USA and UK, universities have highjacked to allow black students and their "woke" allies to literally ban white and non-black (read Asian) students from areas of the campuses and have banned any visiting scholar or author with whom they disagree from coming onto the campus and speak to those interested. No, say the wokeists! Your speech may trigger me and my friends and I don't want to feel uncomfortable so you are banned. The true evil and lunacy here however, is the fact that the Universities go along with it. Now here there is legitimate cause to ban and fire these moronic administrators who allow such a stupendous rejection of the past 250 years of history, leaning, free speech and enlightenment. The Universities of today have become breeding grounds for LGBTQI-AAP+, Transgender, White hysteria, Man hating, Female hating and Lecturer hating luddites. Who, if given the chance, will become the modern Sans Culotte[53] complete with a metaphorical (hopefully) guillotine...

This lunatic fringe of students, educators and administrators need to go. This continued rubbish must stop. We are watching as the, former , great institutions of learning are literally torn down to the "Woke" god. We are not observing society growing and changing organically, we are witnessing the complete destruction of the meritocracy upon which Universities and Colleges were founded. To further prove this point, I have included the text from an Australian Education Magazine. I am embarrassed to do so.

But if you think all this truly malevolent "woke" nonsense only occurs in the USA, the EU, and UK. Think again. The following is from my home, Australia.

---

[53] were the common people of the lower classes in late 18th-century France, a great many of whom became radical and militant partisans of the French Revolution in response to their poor quality of life under the Ancien Régime.[1] The word sans-culotte, which is opposed to that of the aristocrat, seems to have been used for the first time on 28 February 1791 by Jean-Bernard Gauthier de Murnan in a derogatory sense, speaking about a "sans-culottes army".[2] The word came into vogue during the demonstration of 20 June 1792.[3]

179

'Nonsense' calls to rename 'English' in national curriculum 'has to be rejected'

Education Minister Alan Tudge says "it's deeply depressing" that these sort of views "infect" our universities amid calls by an influential university academic to scrap the word 'English' from the national curriculum.
The Courier Mail reports a senior lecturer at the University of Melbourne, Dr Melitta Hogarth called for the subject 'English' to be renamed because it "asserts" the "besieged sovereignty of the colonial state".

Mr Tudge said at the conference Dr Hogarth could've instead talked about a range of other issues such as "how we're going to get these kids back up to speed from months of lost learning" or focused on "indigenous education". "But no, we have to put up with this sort of nonsense, has to be rejected and it's deeply depressing these sort of views infect our leading universities."

Thank reason that the Education Minister is at least a man with half a brain. Miss Hogarth, unbelievably, is an assistant Dean of Education at the University of Melbourne.

What a total disgrace.

HONESTLY

On July 26th, 2021, Bari Weiss[54] released an episode of her strong and amazing podcast, "Honestly". The topic was an interview with Maud Maron, a passionate progressive.

 She was a Planned Parenthood volunteer; a research assistant for a Black Panther leader; a Bernie voter; a public-school parent; and, most

---

[54] Bari Weiss is an American opinion writer and editor. From 2013 until 2017, she was an op-ed and book review editor at The Wall Street Journal. From 2017 to 2020, she was an op-ed staff editor and writer about culture and politics at The New York Times. Since March 1, 2021, she has worked as a regular columnist for Die Welt.

significantly, a public defender who worked for many years at Legal Aid.

But fellow progressives, including her colleagues at Legal Aid, now insist that Maud is racist, that she supports segregation, that she is, despite all appearances to the contrary, a modern version of Bull Connor[55].

How did this happen? Why is Maron being lied about so flagrantly? And why did she recently decide to sue Legal Aid, the institution to which she dedicated her career?

You've probably never heard of Maud Maron. But I think you will be shocked by her story, and inspired by her decision to stand up to a tsunami of lies.

---

[55] Theophilus Eugene "Bull" Connor was an American politician who served as Commissioner of Public Safety for the city of Birmingham, Alabama, for more than two decades. A member of the Democratic Party, he strongly opposed the Civil Rights Movement in the 1960s.

Maron's story gives a good indication of just how difficult it is to think independently and break free of the Manhattan group think, particularly if you want to have any kind of public profile.

Weiss's post contains substantial biographical information about Maron that paints her as being, until recently, a rather typical left-wing Manhattan Democrat. She attended Barnard College (where her activities included acting as an escort for Planned Parenthood) and Cardozo Law School. Her career goal was to be a public defender, and she joined the Legal Aid Society (New York's main public defender organization) right out of law school in 1998. After a lengthy hiatus beginning in 2006 to raise four children, she re-joined Legal Aid in 2017. Her Democratic Party credentials include working for the John Kerry campaign in 2004 and contributing (*"many times"*) to the Bernie Sanders campaign in 2016. Her four kids all attend New York City public schools. She was elected to her local Community Education Council in 2017 and again in 2019. In the recent primary elections in New York, she ran in the Democratic primary for the City Council in her district, which is District 1 (Lower Manhattan).

But the combination of having four kids in the public schools and serving on the Community Education Council put Maron in the position to actually learn what passes for "education" in those quarters these days. By mid-2020, when she had begun her run for the City Council, Maron started to speak out about the racist garbage that is sweeping public

182

education in the City. In July 2020, she published an op-ed in the New York Post with the headline "Racial obsessions make it impossible for NYC schools to treat parents, kids as people." Excerpt:

I am a mom, a public defender, an elected public-school council member and a City Council candidate. But at a city Department of Education anti-bias training, I was instructed to refer to myself as a "white woman" — as if my whole life reduces to my race. Those who oppose this ideology are shunned and humiliated, even as it does nothing to actually improve our broken schools. Though facing severe budget cuts, the DOE has spent more than $6 million for the training, which defines qualities such as "worship of the written word," "individualism" and "objectivity" as "white-supremacy culture." The administration, and many local politicians, buy into a benign-sounding but chilling doctrine called anti-racism, which insists on defining everyone by race, invites discrimination and divides all thought and behaviour along a racial axis.

In short, at least on this one issue where Maron is quite knowledgeable, she had broken from the official Manhattan orthodoxy and groupthink. What next? Undoubtedly, you can guess. From Weiss:

Three days after she published the piece, the Black Attorneys of Legal Aid Caucus put out a lengthy statement saying that "Maud Maron has no business having a career in public defence, and we're ashamed that she works for the Legal Aid Society." It declared: "Maud is racist, and openly so," and offered no evidence to back up the charge. It said that this veteran public defender was a "prominent opponent of equality" and a "classic example of what 21st century racism looks like."

That was the beginning of what Weiss describes as the "witch trial." The statement of Black Attorneys of Legal Aid group [56] was retweeted without comment of the Legal Aid Society itself. Various of Maron's Legal Aid colleagues issued tweets calling her things like a "pathetic racist" with a "segregation platform." Four colleagues published a lengthy attack piece on August 14, 2020 in Gotham Gazette with the headline "When School Segregationist Dog Whistle Becomes a Bull-horn."

Weiss interviewed (or attempted to interview) several of Maron's Legal Aid colleagues for the piece. Exactly one, by the name of James Chubinsky, was willing to speak for attribution; and he has recently retired. Chubinsky, who had been Maron's supervisor in her most recent stint at Legal Aid, called her work performance "beyond terrific." Another colleague had similarly complimentary things to say, but would not allow his name to be used. Chubinsky has this to say about the current environment at Legal Aid:

"It was becoming intolerable," Chubsinky said of the intolerance that had taken root at Legal Aid. "We talked about all of this behind closed doors. Because you can't talk about this with the doors open. It's a really oppressive environment for anyone who isn't radical, including, by the way, those attorneys of colour who don't share these lunatic views like abolishing the police or saying that it's necessarily racist to arrest people for misdemeanour crimes."

---

[56] https://bit.ly/MaudMaron

The latest is that on July 12 Maron filed a lawsuit in Manhattan federal court accusing the Legal Aid Society of racial discrimination against her and of constructive termination.

Here are my comments for Ms. Maron:

I am enormously glad that you have awakened to the harm that left-wing education doctrine is currently inflicting on schools, children and parents. I am also enormously glad that you have decided that this issue is sufficiently important that you are willing to speak out about it at substantial risk to your career and standing among your peers.

But on the other hand, where are you now, and where have you been for the last 25 years (since you graduated from college) on the rest of the destructive agenda of the left? You supported Bernie Sanders in the 2016 election. Did you somehow miss that this guy was a cheerleader for the Soviet Union until right up to the time of its collapse, and that he remains a supporter of the Castro regime in Cuba to this day? The essence of these regimes, and of the socialism that Sanders explicitly advocates for, is the very sort of suppression of dissent that you are now experiencing. Were you somehow unable to learn about or understand how this works, and why it is so evil, until it actually happened to you personally?

Having read about the New York City public education from insiders, many of whom have been subjected to its "white supremacy" training, you now know how destructive the policies of the left are in this one area. But are you willing to take any time to investigate and apply any scepticism in other areas? For example, Weiss quotes you as saying *"If you had asked me when I became a mom what I thought were the pressing concerns my kids would face I probably would have said climate change . . . "* Have you taken any time since then to educate yourself on that subject? Or are you just going along with the trendy orthodoxy and groupthink until it completely destroys our economy and impoverishes all the low income people?

Anyway, once again welcome, at least in part, to the side of rationality.

Finally, I note that Ms. Maron got approximately 9% of the vote in the recent City Council primary in her district, which was good enough for a fourth place finish. It appears that she will now run again in November as an Independent.

The Storm clouds aren't just gathering, they have moved in to stay; unless we do something.

THE PERFERVID[57] LEFT

It is a sad reality of Wokeists that many of their high priests are appalling speakers; frantic, illiterate, extreme and fanatical. Prone to exaggeration and inflammation, these perfervid folk seem to intentionally poison their own message by the use of extreme language and falsehoods in an attempt to agitate their disciples. They spread their indoctrination through extremism, violence, intolerance and racism. All forged in the crucible of extreme Marxism and narcissism. Chief amongst them is poorly educated and sadly unintelligent congresswoman from New York City; Alexandria Ocasio-Cortes, who models herself as "AOC", is further left than Bernie Sanders and harbours delusions of grandeur so great that she appears, at times, to be a foil for the egotism of Donald Trump. Just another example of the confusion and division that is going on today in the once United States.

Mind you, there is no shortage of ego amongst the world's politicians and hangers-on these days. From Dr. Fauci, who has shown himself to be a liar and a media hog, to Andrew Cuomo and his joke of a brother and CNN anchor, to Nancy Pelosi, the 80 year old speaker of the House to Jens Stoltenberg, the stunningly unpopular ex-prime minister of Norway who was surprisingly and stunningly appointed to the position of the Secretary General of NATO, and who was given the job only a week after Obama received his Nobel Peace Prize, ironically awarded by the Norwegian Nobel committee. The corruption of our world leaders is

---

[57] Perfervid: marked by overwrought or exaggerated emotion : excessively fervent. Violent reaction to something trivial.

187

extraordinary and quite convincing evidence of the complete useless-
ness of politicians and our failed democratic systems.

The world is truly in a unique and most odd situation in this modern era.
Media has become utterly useless as it fails to report the truth but cease-
lessly offers up opinion and bias.

All intelligent and motivated people need to speak up against the lunacy
of this angry, under educated and over socialised minority. I do not
mean the Black people. In a recent CBS poll in the US, 82% of black
males reject the BLM movement and all its hypocrisy. They recognise
it as Marxism in the extreme and all thinking people should know to
reject that. There are no end of examples of cultural Marxism devouring
its own adherents and disciples. I can only hope that the Ouroboros
continues its vital work and that the lunatic fringe will be shouted down
by reason and bring about a new and sustainable Age of Enlightenment.

---

*The move from a structuralist account in which capital is understood to structure social
relations in relatively homologous ways to a view of hegemony in which power relations are subject to repetition, convergence, and rearticulation brought the question
of temporality into the thinking of structure, and marked a shift from a form of Al-
thusserian[58] theory that takes structural totalities as theoretical objects to one in which
the insights into the contingent possibility of structure inaugurate a renewed*

---

[58] Louis Pierre Althusser was a French Marxist philosopher.

conception of hegemony as bound up with the contingent sites and strategies of the rearticulation of power. Judith Butler[59]

Judith Butler
Main Interests listed as: Feminist Theory, Political Philosophy, Ethics, Psychoanalysis, Phenomenology, Discourse, Embodiment, Sexuality, Gender Theory, Jewish Philosophy.

The above text is a quote from an American Philosopher and Educator. Obviously, she has completely ignored the concept of writing; for normal people to comprehend. Pompous and unnecessarily verbose, this is a classic example of the Wokeist Manifesto in action. Use big words, say nothing and everyone will agree and think you're brilliant.

Well, not this bunny, and not my readers.

We just think you are arrogant and pompous and your ridiculous use of un-common words simply shows that your obfuscating style demonstrates that you do not wish to be understood. All of which, sets you out to be a complete fraud, albeit with an impressive, but fundamentally useless vocabulary.

---

[59] Judith Pamela Butler (born February 24, 1956) is an American philosopher, strict Marxist and gender theorist whose work has influenced political philosophy, ethics, and the fields of third-wave feminism, queer theory, and literary theory while totally obfuscating everything she publishers to try to appear intelligent.

A NEW ENLIGHTENMENT

It's time for a new enlightenment. Reason and Democracy have fled our modern transom and era. We've played with them, stretched them, analysed them and ignored them; and now we've broken them…possibly beyond repair.

The idea of the meritocracy, is also dead. If the ideas pursued by some in the Political, Scientific, Cultural, Educational fields get their way, then everything will about affirmative action and quotas. Not merit. Orchestras will end up being very representative of current cultural and ethnic demographics, but their standard may very well be adversely affected. Orchestras are selected purely on Merit. In fact these days most auditions are blind. Which means that they are performed behind a screen or curtain. Speaking is not permitted. How on earth would affirmative action aide in this process?

Francis Collins, the brilliant physician, geneticist, who led the Human Genome Project for many years and is the current head of the National Institute of Health in the USA; has stated that he refuses to attend any more medical conferences unless the attendees and speakers are at least 50% female and 20% black. What a complete disgrace and an abandonment of his responsibility to society and to Medicine. It should also be incredibly insulting to women. And Black people. This is just one example of the death of the enlightenment. Sacrificing Merit on an altar of Gender or Race does not provide an adequate platform for artificially enforced diversity of intersectionality.

What if we did the same "balancing" trick the other way and forced NBA teams to have a minimum of 50% white players. Or country and western music that must release 30% of their albums by Asian musicians.

When it comes to anything that is focused on the achievement of excellence, forced diversity and equity will simply kill off the endeavour completely. A famous American Football coach once said; "Adequacy in the pursuit of excellence, is unacceptable." Damn right it is. It should be. We need it to be. I don't want my brain surgeon or oncologist to have received his or her position through a diversity and equity quota. I want the very best surgeon no matter what the colour of his or her skin might be or what gender they were born with and what label they say that they identify with. I don't want identity politics to play a role at all. Not in my surgeon, or my music, or my society or even sport (which frankly, I couldn't care less about).

I don't want to be told that I have to live in a society where everyone is divided by their race and gender and identity. I want a Martin Luther King world where we are all judged by the content of our character and not the colour of our skin. I thought that we pretty much had that before all this garbage started. Gay people are more and more accepted and the battle for Gay Rights has pretty much been won. Woman are no longer living in a male world. I will agree that there is still the "boys club" feel to every organisation that I have ever worked for but 3 out of 4 of them also have woman in very senior position as well.

I don't think woman are oppressed, I don't think that white people are all racist and evil oppressors, I do not concede that there is any such thing as Male Fragility or Toxicity. To even suggest such nonsense is to deny individuality at its core. There is no such thing as the LGBT community. There are most certainly people who live a different life style than me. But they not homogenous. A Large group of individuals are not all the same to any degree.

There is no such thing as the Black Community either. The percentage of people who live in our society and are of African or Caribbean or any place with a dark skinned people. They are not homogenous either. They are not all the same. They share a common characteristic of higher levels of melatonin in their skin and some minor facial characteristic differences. That does not a community make.

What led to the first Age of Enlightenment? 1650 – 1800

There are some very significant factors that led to the first Enlightenment. Perhaps the most obvious is that the previous 1000 years had been full of Wars, Inquisitions, Religious upheaval, Scientific and Mathematical breakthroughs, Plagues and Rebellions etc. It was not a great time to be alive. Certainly compared to today it was Short, Dirty and Terrible. Then around 1650 things started to slowly change. Medicine and Science where challenging the Church for ownership of community psyche. The Dominion of the Church had been rocked by the 30 years' war (1618-1648) leading to the Protestant Reformation. All over Europe, there were signs of dramatic change and growth.

French cultural leadership in the eighteenth century was preeminent. The key concepts of the eighteenth-century philosophes, or intellectuals, were reason, natural law, and progress. Philosophes, who expressed optimism in human abilities to apply reason, owed a debt to John Locke for their ideas on government and human psychology.

Under the direction of Diderot, philosophes produced the thirty-three-volume Emyclopédie, advancing views of progress and reason, exposing superstition and ignorance, and denouncing inequality in the light of natural law and science.

Francois Quesnay and Adam Smith summed up the economic principles of those philosophes known as Physiocrats. The Physiocrat's program of laissez faire, or "let nature take its course," clashed with traditional mercantilist doctrines.

In justice and education, philosophes sought reforms based on reason and natural law. They championed tolerance and attacked superstition. The well-known philosophe Voltaire professed belief in God but rejected intolerance and furthered deist doctrine.

Like many other philosophes, Montesquieu in The Spirit of the Laws (1748) expressed admiration for British ideas on government. In The

Social Contract[60] (1762), Jean-Jacques Rousseau set out his theory of the general will to reconcile the needs of the individual and the institution of government. Rousseau's ideas have formed the basis of radical political doctrines ever since.

Enlightened despots of the period displayed a mix of Enlightenment ideas and absolute monarchy. Frederick the Great read the works of philosophes and promoted Physiocratic ideas in agriculture. But he rejected laissez- faire ideas. In religion and social policy, he inaugurated a measure of tolerance and supported judicial reforms but did not move to reduce social inequality.

Joseph II of Austria, Charles III of Spain, as well as rulers in Portugal and Sweden instituted enlightened reforms. However, the successors of these enlightened rulers did not continue their programs.

In Russia, Catherine, The Great, was an absolute autocrat who liked the idea of reform. She tried to codify laws based on enlightened ideas, reorganized local government, and introduced some municipal reform. But under Catherine, serfdom grew as the nobility gained increased authority over their serfs.

Czar Alexander I had absorbed enlightened ideas but was hesitant and accomplished little despite good intentions. Russia continued its

---

[60] The Social Contract (Appendix I)

expansionist foreign policy. Catherine annexed the Crimea and participated in the partitions of Poland.

In Britain, George III, stubborn and short-sighted, tried to reassert royal prerogative. After the Seven Years' War, a breach divided Britain and its North American colonies. Colonists' resistance to Britain's attempt to raise revenue in North America resulted in the issuing of the Declaration of Independence on July 4, 1776.

With French help, the colonists won their independence, which was recognized in 1783 at the Peace of Paris. The successful revolt of the American colonists weakened the power and prestige of George III. The Declaration of Independence appealed to the laws of nature described by Locke, while the new Constitution of the United States reflected Montesquieu's ideas on the separation of powers.

Philosophes failed to take into account the complexities of human nature. Their appeals to the laws of nature and reason did not reform states. David Hume and Immanuel Kant reflected the philosophic reaction to rationalism. Popular reaction to the Enlightenment was expressed in German Pietism and the Methodist movement in England.

A new type of fiction appeared in the works of Daniel Defoe and the social novels of Henry Fielding. In Germany, Goethe's Sorrows of Young Werther embodied the frustration of the Sturm and Drang[61]

---

[61] a style or movement of German literature of the latter half of the 18th century: characterized chiefly by impetuosity of manner, exaltation of individual sensibility

movement. Neoclassicism influenced the arts, but the age of romanticism was foreshadowed in the growing taste for the oriental, natural, and Gothic.

Europe and the known world was poised for what came as part of this movement. The Age of Revolution.

The **Age of Revolution** is a period from the late 18th to the mid-19th centuries in which a number of significant revolutionary movements occurred in most of Europe and the Americas. The period is noted for the change from absolutist monarchies to representative governments with a written constitution, and the creation of nation states.

Influenced by the new ideas of the Enlightenment, the American Revolution (1765–1783) is usually considered the starting point of the Age of Revolution. It in turn inspired the French Revolution of 1789, which rapidly spread to the rest of Europe through its wars. In 1799, Napoleon took power in France and continued the French Revolutionary Wars by conquering most of continental Europe. Although Napoleon imposed on his conquests several modern concepts such as equality before the law, or a civil code, his rigorous military occupation triggered national rebellions, notably in Spain and Germany. After Napoleon's defeat, European great powers forged the Holy Alliance at the Congress of Vienna in 1814–15, in an attempt to prevent future revolutions, and also restored the previous monarchies. Nevertheless, Spain was

---

and intuitive perception, opposition to established forms of society and thought, and extreme nationalism.

considerably weakened by the Napoleonic Wars and could not control its American colonies, almost all of which proclaimed their independence between 1810 and 1820. Revolution then spread back to southern Europe in 1820, with uprisings in Portugal, Spain, Italy, and Greece. Continental Europe was shaken by two similar revolutionary waves in 1830 and 1848, also called the Spring of Nations. The democratic demands of the revolutionaries often merged with independence or national unification movements, such as in Italy, Germany, Poland, Hungary, etc. The violent repression of the Springtime of Nations marked the end of the era.

The Spring of Nations

The Revolutions of 1848, known in some countries as the Springtime of the Peoples or the Springtime of Nations, were a series of political upheavals throughout Europe in 1848. It remains the most widespread revolutionary wave in European history.

The revolutions were essentially democratic and liberal in nature, with the aim of removing the old monarchical structures and creating independent nation-states. The revolutions spread across Europe after an initial revolution began in France in February. Over 50 countries were affected, but with no significant coordination or cooperation among their respective revolutionaries. Some of the major contributing factors were widespread dissatisfaction with political leadership, demands for more participation in government and democracy, demands for freedom of the press, other demands made by the working class, the upsurge of nationalism, the regrouping of established government forces, and the European Potato Failure, which triggered mass starvation, migration, and civil unrest.

The 1848 Revolutions were a product of, and a reaction to, the "isms:" Nationalism, Liberalism, Conservatism, Militarism, and so on.

Does it sound familiar? Can we draw parallels to the bizarre workings of the Wokeists today. The death of Free Speech, the irrelevance of the media due to their bias, lack of transparent honesty and the advent of Identity Politics in all its guises and flavours, Transgenderism,

Am I advocating for revolution? Yes. But not a violent and bloody one at all.

Revolution to achieve the new enlightenment can be achieved peacefully and in the purest form of Ghandi-ism.

- Reject Critical Race Theory completely.
- Reject Male Toxicity as a concept.
- Reject White Fragility as a concept.
- Reject Paediatric Gender Reassignment without parental consent.
- Reject far left policies and Marxist ideology and tell your politicians that you don't want it
- Vote out all politicians who do not respect the will of the people
- Have a serious think about politicians still serving into their 80's and vote them out too.

- Reject Marxism totally, as the rest of the world did 100 years ago.
- Ok, Cuba and Venezuela haven't rejected it yet…but I'm hopeful.
- Oppose the obscene and destructive power of the papacy but support personal faith.
- Observe values that are important and reject the ideologies that you have adopted over the past 5 years to keep your job and not get cancelled.

So, what am I saying with this book and this chapter.

Think for yourself. Reject crowd mentality and mob rule. Place value on the achievements of all people. White, Black, Brown, Orange, Lilac, Magenta. I don't care what colour anybody is, what gender they or frankly even what they identify as. But do not teach any child that they are less important or more important. Do not lose the English language to the idiocrasy of "Language Art". Stop talking about any group of people as a monolithic "community". There is no such thing. We 7.6 Billion people who are all valid, all valuable, all worthy of their own unique identity if they wish.

But stop pushing your ridiculous, unproven, maniacal, totalitarian BULLSHIT down everybody's throat. Take your cancel culture and shove it. Take you Facebook and Twitter and Google cancelling and banning and shove that as well. Universities belong to everyone not just the bleeding heart minority of ratbags that run them today. Support strong people and help them to be strong in the hellish world the Wokeists are trying to make us live in.

All in all, think for yourself, expand your horizons, feed your mind and love those dear to you.

What else can anyone do?

THE END

APPENDICES

(PWS: A little light reading for those that may be interested.)

1: ROUSSEAU 1762

THE SOCIAL CONTRACT

Excerpt from

The Social Contract Jean-Jacques Rousseau

OR PRINCIPLES OF POLITICAL RIGHT 1762

Translated by G. D. H. Cole, public domain

Foederis æquas Dicamus leges. Virgil, Æneid xi.

GLOSSARY

agreement: The item that Rousseau calls a *convention* is an event, whereas what we call 'conventions' (setting aside the irrelevant 'convention' = 'professional get-together') are not events but enduring states of affairs like the conventions governing the meanings of words, the standards of politeness, etc. So 'convention' is a wrong translation; and 'agreement' is right.

alienate: To alienate something that you own is to bring it about that you no longer own it; in brief, to give it away or sell it,

arbitrary: It means 'brought into existence by the decision of some person(s)'. It's no part of the meaning here (as it is today) that the decision was frivolous or groundless.

censorship: This translates Rousseau's *censure*. It doesn't refer to censorship as we know it today; *censure* didn't have that meaning until the 19th century. Rousseau's topic is a role those certain officials had in some periods of the Roman republic, namely as guardians of, and spokesmen for, the people's *mœurs* (see below). They could be thought of as an institutionalising of the 'court of public opinion'. On page 67 we see him stretching the original sense.

compact, contract: These translate Rousseau's *pacte* and *contrat* respectively. He seems to mean them as synonyms.

constitution: In this work a thing's 'constitution' is the sum of facts about how something is *constituted*, how its parts hang together and work together (so the constitution of a state is nothing like a document). Items credited with 'constitutions' are organisms and political entities; the mention on page 66 of the constitution of *a people* seems aberrant.

magistrate: In this work, as in general in early modern times, a 'magistrate' is anyone with an official role in govern- ment. The magistracy is the set of all such officials, thought of as a single body.

mœurs: The *mœurs* of a people include their morality, their basic customs, their attitudes and expectations about how people will behave, their ideas about what is decent. . . and so on. This word—rhyming approximately with 'worse'—is left untranslated because there's no good English equivalent to it. English speakers sometimes use it, for the sort of reason they have for sometimes using *Schadenfreude*.

moral person: Something that isn't literally a person but is being regarded as one for some theoretical purpose. See for example pages 9 and 36.

populace: Rousseau repeatedly speaks of a 'people' in the singular, and we can do that in English ('The English—what a strange people!'); but it many cases this way of using 'people' sounds strained and peculiar, and this version takes refuge in 'populace'. On page 4, for instance, that saves us from 'In every generation the people was the master. . . '.

prince: As was common in his day, Rousseau uses 'prince' to stand for the chief of the government. This needn't be a person with the rank of Prince; it needn't be a person at all, because it could be a committee.

sovereign: This translates *souverain*. As Rousseau makes clear on page 7, he uses this term as a label for the person or group of persons holding supreme power in a state. In a democracy, the whole people constitute a sovereign, and individual citizens are members of the sovereign. In Books 3 and 4 'sovereign' is used for the legislator (or legislature) as distinct from the government = the executive.

subsistence: What is needed for survival—a minimum of food, drink, shelter etc.

wise: An inevitable translation of *sage*, but the meaning in French carries ideas of 'learned', 'scholarly', 'intellectually able', rather more strongly than whatever it is that you and I mean by 'wise'.

you, we: When this version has Rousseau speaking of what 'you' or 'we' may do, he has spoken of what 'one' may do. It is normal idiomatic French to use *on* = 'one' much oftener than we can use 'one' in English without sounding stilted (Fats Waller: 'One never knows, do one?').

BOOK I

This little treatise is salvaged from a much longer work that I abandoned long ago, having started it without thinking about whether I was capable of pulling it off. Of various bits that might be rescued from what I had written of that longer work, what I offer here is the most substantial and, it seems to me, the least unworthy of being published. None of the rest of it is.

I plan to address this question: With men as they are and with laws as they could be, can there be in the civil order any sure and legitimate rule of administration? In tackling this I shall try always to unite •what *right* allows with •what *interest* demands, so that •justice and •utility don't at any stage part company.

I start on this without showing that the subject is important. You may want to challenge me: 'So you want to write on politics—are you then a prince [see Glossary] or a legislator?' I answer that I am neither, and that is why I write on politics. If I were a prince or a legislator I wouldn't waste my time *saying* what should be done; I would *do* it, or keep quiet.

As I was born a citizen of a free state, and am a member of its sovereign [see Glossary], my right to vote makes it my duty to study public affairs, however little influence my voice can have on them. Happily, when I think about governments I always find that my inquiries give me new reasons for loving the government of my own country!

I. THE SUBJECT OF THE FIRST BOOK

Man is born free, and everywhere he is in chains. Here's one who thinks he is the master of others, yet he is more enslaved than they are. How did this change come about? I don't know. What can make it legitimate? That's a question that I think I can answer.

If I took into account nothing but force and what can be done by force, I would say:

"As long as a people is constrained to obey, it does well to obey; as soon as it can shake off the yoke, it does even better to shake it off. ·If its right to do so is challenged, it can answer that·: it gets its liberty back by the same 'right'—·namely, force·—that took it away in the first place. Any justification for taking it away equally justifies taking it back; and if there was no justification for its being taken away ·no justification for taking it back is called for·."

But the social order ·isn't to be understood in terms of force; it· is a sacred right on which all other rights are based. But it doesn't come from nature, so it must be based on agreements. Before coming to that, though, I have to establish the truth of what I have been saying.

2. THE FIRST SOCIETIES

The most ancient of all societies, and the only *natural* one, is the society of the family. Yet the children remain attached to the father only for as long as they need him for their preservation; as soon as this need ceases, the natural bond is dissolved. The children, released from the obedience they owed to the father, and the father, released from the care he owed his children, return equally to independence. If they remain united, this is something they do not •naturally but •voluntarily, and the family itself is then maintained only by agreement.

This common liberty is an upshot of the nature of man. His first law is to provide for his own preservation, his first cares are those he owes to himself; and as soon as he can think for himself he is the sole judge of the right way to take care of himself, which makes him his own master.

You could call the family the *prime model* of political societies: the ruler corresponds to the father, and the people to the children; and all of them—·ruler, people, father, children·—because they were born free and equal don't give up their liberty without getting something in return. The whole difference is that •in the family the father's care for his children is repaid by his love for them, whereas •in the state the ruler's care for the people under him is repaid not by love for them (which he doesn't have!) but by the pleasure of being in charge.

Grotius denies that all human power is established in favour of the governed, and cites slavery as a counterexample. His usual method of reasoning is to establish •right by •fact [meaning: . . . 'to draw conclusions about what should be the case from premises about what is the case']. Not the most logical of argument-patterns, but it's one that is very favourable to tyrants.

. . . .Throughout his book, Grotius seems to favour—as does Hobbes—the thesis that the human species is divided into so many herds of cattle, each with a ruler who keeps guard over them for the purpose of devouring them.

Philo tells us that the Emperor Caligula reasoned thus: As a shepherd has a higher nature than his flock does, so also the shepherds of men, i.e. their rulers, have a higher nature than do the peoples under them; from which he inferred, reasonably enough, that either kings were gods or men were beasts.

This reasoning of Caligula's is on a par with that of Hobbes and Grotius. Aristotle, before any of them, had said that men are not naturally equal because some are born for slavery and others for command.

Aristotle was right; but he mistook the effect for the cause. Every man born *in* slavery is born *for* slavery—nothing is more certain than that. Slaves lose everything in their chains, even the desire to escape from them: they love their servitude, as Ulysses' comrades loved their brutish condition ·when the goddess Circe turned them into pigs·. So if there *are* slaves *by* nature, that's because there *have been* slaves *against* nature. Force made the first slaves, and their cowardice kept them as slaves.

I have said nothing about King Adam; or about Emperor Noah, the father of three great monarchs who shared out the universe (like Saturn's children, whom some scholars have recognised in them). I hope to be given credit for my moderation: as a direct descendant of one of these princes—perhaps of the eldest branch—I don't know that a verification of titles wouldn't show me to be the legitimate king of the human race! Anyway, Adam was undeniably sovereign of the world, as Robinson Crusoe was of his island, as long as he was its only inhabitant; and this empire had the advantage that the monarch, safe on his throne, had nothing to fear from rebellions, wars, or conspirators.

3. THE RIGHT OF THE STRONGEST

The strongest is never strong enough to be always the master unless he transforms •strength into •right, and •obedience into •duty. Hence 'the right of the strongest'—a phrase that one might think is meant ironically, but is actually laid down as a basic truth. But will no-one ever *explain* this phrase? Force is a physical power; I don't see what moral effect it can have. Giving way to force is something you have to do, not something you choose to do; ·or if you insist that choice comes into it·, it is at most an act of *prudence*. In what sense can it be a *duty*?

Suppose for a moment that this so-called 'right ·of the strongest·' exists. I maintain that we'll get out of this nothing but a mass of inexplicable nonsense. If force makes right, then if you change the force you change the right (effects change when causes change!), so that when one force overcomes another, there's a corresponding change in what is right. The moment it becomes possible to disobey •with impunity it becomes possible to disobey •legitimately. And because the strongest are always in the right, the only thing that matters is to work to become the strongest. Now, what sort of right is it that perishes when force fails? If force *makes* us obey, we can't be morally obliged to obey; and if force doesn't make us obey, then ·on the theory we are examining· we are under no obligation to do so. Clearly, the word 'right' adds nothing to force: in this context it doesn't stand for anything.

'Obey the powers that be.' If this means submit to force, it is a good precept, but superfluous: I guarantee that it will never be violated! All power comes from God, I admit; but so does all sickness—are we then forbidden to send for the doctor? A robber confronts me at the edge of a wood: I am compelled to hand over my money, but is it the case that even if I *could* hold onto it I am morally obliged to hand it over? After all, the pistol he holds is also a power.

Then let us agree that force doesn't create right, and that legitimate powers are the only ones we are obliged to obey. Which brings us back to my original question.

4. SLAVERY

Since no man has a natural authority over his fellow, and force creates no right, we are left with •agreements [see Glossary] as the basis for all legitimate authority among men.

Grotius says:

"If an individual can alienate [see Glossary] his liberty and make himself the slave of a master, why couldn't a whole people alienate its liberty and make itself subject to a king?"

This contains several ambiguous words that need to be explained, but let us confine ourselves to 'alienate'. To alienate something is to give or sell it. Now, a man who becomes the slave of another does not *give* himself—he *sells* himself at the rock-bottom price of his subsistence [see Glossary]. But when a people sells itself what price is paid? ·Not their subsistence:· Far from providing his subjects with their subsistence, a king gets his own subsistence only from them. . . . Do subjects then give

210

their persons on condition that the king takes their goods also? I fail to see what they have left to preserve.

'The despot guarantees civic peace in the state', you may say. Granted; but what do the people gain if the wars his ambition brings down on them, his insatiable greed, and harassments by his ministers bring them more misery than they'd have suffered from their own dissensions ·if no monarchy had been established·? What do they gain if this *peace* is one of their miseries? You can live peacefully in a dungeon, but does that make it a good life? The Greeks imprisoned in the cave of the Cyclops lived there peacefully while waiting for their turn to be eaten.

To say that a man *gives* himself ·to someone else, i.e. hands himself over· *free*, is to say something absurd and inconceivable; such an act is null and illegitimate, simply because the man who does it is out of his mind. To say the same of a whole people is to suppose a *people* of madmen; and madness doesn't create any right.

Even if each man could alienate himself, he couldn't alienate his children: they are born men, and born free; their liberty belongs to them, and no-one else has the right to dispose of it. While they are too young to decide for themselves, their father can, in their name, lay down conditions for their preservation and well-being; but he can't make an irrevocable and unconditional *gift* of them; such a gift is contrary to the ends of nature, and exceeds the rights of paternity. So an arbitrary [see Glossary] government couldn't be legitimate unless in every generation

211

the populace [see Glossary] was the master who was in a position to accept or reject it; but then the government would no longer be arbitrary!

To renounce your liberty is to renounce •your status as a man, •your rights as a human being, and even •your duties as a human being. There can't be any way of compensating someone who gives up everything. Such a renunciation is incompatible with man's nature; to remove all freedom from his will is to remove all morality from his actions. Finally, an 'agreement' to have absolute authority on one side and unlimited obedience on the other—what an empty and contradictory agreement that would have to be! Isn't it clear that if we are entitled to take anything and everything from a person, we can't be under any obligation to him? And isn't that fact alone—the fact that there is no equivalence, nothing to be exchanged, between the two sides—enough to nullify the 'agreement'? What right can my slave have against me? Everything that he has is mine; his right is mine; and it doesn't make sense to speak of my right against myself.

Grotius and company cite *war* as another source for the so-called right of slavery. The winner having (they say) the right to kill the loser, the latter can buy back his life at the price of his freedom; and this agreement is all the more legitimate in being to the advantage of both parties.

But this supposed right to kill the loser is clearly not an upshot of the state of war. Men are not *naturally* one another's enemies. Any natural relations amongst them must exist when they are living in their primitive independence without any government or social structure; but at

212

that time they have no inter-relations that are stable enough to constitute either the state of peace or the state of war. War is constituted by a relation between things, not between persons; and because the state of war can't arise out of simple personal relations but only out of thing-relations, there can't be a private war (a war of man against man) in the state of nature, where there is no ownership, or in the state of society, where everything is under the authority of the laws.

Individual combats, duels and encounters are acts that can't constitute a state. As for the private wars that were authorised by Louis IX of France. . . ., they were abuses of feudal government, which was itself an absurd system if ever there was one—contrary to the principles of natural right and to all good government.

So war is a relation not between man and man but between state and state, and individuals are enemies only accidentally, not as •men nor even as •citizens but as •soldiers; not as belonging to their country but as defenders of it.[1] And the only enemies a state can have are other states; not men, because there can't be a real settled relation between things as radically different as states and men.

This principle squares with the established rules of all times and the constant practice of all civilised peoples. Declarations of war don't give notice to •powers as much as to •their subjects. A foreigner—whether king, individual, or whole people—who robs, kills or detains the subjects ·of a country· without first declaring war on their prince is not an enemy but a bandit. When a full-scale war is going on, a prince is entitled to help himself to anything in the enemy country that belongs to the public, but if he is just he will respect the lives and goods of individuals—he will respect rights on which his own are based. The purpose of the war is to destroy the enemy state, so we [see Glossary] have a right to kill its defenders while they are bearing arms; but as soon as they lay down their weapons and surrender, they stop being enemies or instruments of the enemy and resume their status as simply *men*, and no-one has any right to take their lives. Sometimes it is possible to kill a state without killing any of its members; and a war doesn't give any right that isn't *needed* for the war to gain its objective. These principles are not those of Grotius: they aren't based on the authority of poets, but are derived from the nature of things and are based on reason.

What about the 'right of conquest'? The only basis for that is 'the law of the strongest'! If war doesn't give the winner the right to massacre the conquered peoples, you can't cite *that* right—a 'right' that doesn't exist—as a basis for a right to enslave those peoples. No-one has a right to kill an enemy except when he can't make him a slave, so the right to enslave him can't be derived from the right to kill him: it's not fair dealing to make him spend his freedom so as to keep his life, over which the victor holds no right. Isn't it clear that there's a vicious circle in basing the right of life and death on the right of slavery, and the right of slavery on the right of life and death?

Even if we assume this terrible right to kill everybody, I maintain that someone enslaved in war isn't committed to do anything for his master except what he is compelled to do; and the same goes for a conquered

214

people. [Rousseau's point here is that the enslaved individual or the conquered people doesn't *owe* the conqueror anything.] By taking an equivalent for his life, the winner hasn't done him a favour; instead of killing him without profit, he has killed him usefully. He is indeed so far from getting any •authority over the slave in addition to his •power over him, that the two are still in a state of war towards one another: their master/slave relation comes from that, and this enforcement of a right of war doesn't imply that there has been a peace-treaty! They have reached an agreement; but this agreement, far from ending the state of war, presupposes its continuance.

Whatever angle we look at it from, therefore, the 'right of slavery' is null and void—not only as illegitimate but also as absurd and meaningless. The words 'slave' and 'right' contradict each other, and are mutually exclusive. It will always be crazy to say to a man, or to a people: "I make an agreement with you wholly at your expense and wholly to my advantage; I shall keep it as long as I like, and you will keep it as long as I like." allowed to serve as a volunteer without explicitly agreeing to serve against such-and-such a named enemy. [Rousseau throws in an anecdote about a soldier whose military oath had to be renewed because etc. He continues:] I know that the siege of Clusium[62] and other isolated events can be cited against me; but I'm talking ·not about individual episodes, but· about laws and customs. The Romans obeyed their laws

---

[62] Clusium is a battle that took place in June of 82 BC during the Roman Republic's Second Civil War. The battle pitted the Optimates under the command of Lucius Cornelius Sulla against the Populares commanded by Gnaeus Papirius Carbo. The battle was indecisive.

more than any other people, and they had better laws than any other people.

5. WE MUST ALWAYS GO BACK TO A FIRST AGREEMENT

[For 'agreement' see Glossary.] Even if I granted everything that I have refuted up to here, the supporters of despotism would be no better off. Ruling a society will always be a quite different thing from subduing a multitude. If any number of scattered individuals were successively enslaved by one man, all I can see there is a master and his slaves, and certainly not a people and its ruler. It's a •cluster, if you will, but not an •association; there's no public good there, and no body politic. This man may have enslaved half the world but he is still only an individual; his interest, apart from that of others, is never anything but a purely private interest. When this man dies, the empire he leaves behind him will remains scattered and without unity, like an oak that falls into a fire and dissolves into a heap of ashes when the fire has consumed it.

A people, says Grotius, can give itself to a king; so he must hold that a people is *a people* before it gives itself to a king. This gift is itself a civic act, which has to arise from public deliberation. Before we examine **(2)** the act by which a people gives itself to a king, let's examine **(1)** the act by which the people became a people; for **(1)** must occur before **(2)**, so that **(1)** is the true foundation of society.

Indeed, if there were no prior agreement, what would give the minority any obligation to submit to the choice of the majority (unless the election was unanimous)? A hundred men want to have a master; what gives them the right to vote on behalf of ten who don't? The law of majority voting is itself something established by agreement, and it presupposes that on at least one occasion there was a unanimous vote.

6. THE SOCIAL COMPACT

Let us take it that men have reached the point at which the obstacles to their survival in the state of nature overpower each individual's resources for maintaining himself in that state. So this primitive condition can't go on; the human race will perish unless it changes its manner of existence.

Now, men can't create new forces; they can only •bring together ones that already exist, and •steer them. So their only way to preserve themselves is to unite a number of forces so that they are jointly powerful enough to deal with the obstacles. They have to bring these forces into play in such a way that they act together in a single thrust.

For forces to *add up* in this way, many people have to work together. But each man's force and liberty are what he chiefly needs for his own survival; so how can he put them into this collective effort without harming his own interests and neglecting the care he owes to himself? This difficulty, in the version of it that arises for my present subject, can be put like this:

Find a form of association that will bring the whole common force to bear on defending and protecting each associate's person and goods, doing this in such a way that each of them, while uniting himself with all, still obeys only himself and remains as free as before.

There's the basic problem that is solved by the social contract. [This is the work's first occurrence of that phrase.]

The clauses of this contract are so settled by the nature of the act that the slightest change would make them null and void; so that although they may never have been explicitly stated, they are everywhere the same and everywhere tacitly accepted and recognised, until the social compact [see Glossary] is violated and each individual regains his •original rights and resumes his •natural liberty, while losing the liberty-by-agreement which had been his reason for renouncing •them.

Properly understood, these clauses come down to one— the total alienation [see Glossary] of each associate, together with all his rights, to the whole community. ·This may seem drastic, but three features of it make it reasonable·. (i) Because each individual gives himself *entirely*, what is happening here for any one individual is the same as what is happening for each of the others, and, because this is so, no-one has any interest in making things tougher for everyone but himself.

(ii) Because the alienation is made without reserve, ·i.e. without anything being held back·, the union is as complete as it can be, and no associate has anything more to demand. ·To see why the association *has to* be done in this way, consider· what the situation would be if the individuals retained certain rights. In the absence of any superior to decide issues about this, each individual would be his own judge in the first case that came up, and this would lead him to ask to be his own judge across the board; this would continue the state of nature, and the association would necessarily become inoperative or tyrannical.

Each man in giving himself to everyone gives himself to no-one; and •the right over himself that the others get is matched by •the right that he gets over each of them. So he gains as much as he loses, and *also* gains extra force for the preservation of what he has.

Filtering out the inessentials, we'll find that the social compact comes down to this:

"Each of us puts his person and all his power in common under the supreme direction of the general will, and, in our corporate capacity, we receive each member as an indivisible part of the whole."

This act of association instantly replaces •the individual- person status of each contracting party by •a moral and collective body, composed of as many members as the assembly has *voix* [= 'voices' or 'votes']; and receiving from this act its unity, its common identity, its life and its will. This public person that is formed by the union of all the other persons used to be called a 'city',[2] and these days is called a 'republic' or a 'body politic'. Its members call it

a *'state'* when thinking of it as passive,

a *'sovereign'* when thinking of it as active, and

a *'power'* when setting it alongside others of the same kind.

Those who are associated in it are collectively called 'a people', and are separately called 'citizens' (as sharing in the sovereign power) and 'subjects' (as being under the state's laws. But these terms are often muddled and confused with one another: it is enough to know how to distinguish them when they are being used with precision.

The real meaning of 'city' has been almost wholly lost in modern times; most people mistake a town for a city, and a townsman for a citizen. They don't know that houses make a town, but citizens a city. . . . I have never read of the title 'citizens' being given to the subjects of any prince, not even the ancient Macedonians or the English of today, though they are nearer liberty than anyone else. Only the French casually adopt the label 'citizens'; that's because they have no idea of its real meaning (you can see that from their dictionaries!). . . . They think of the name as expressing *a virtue rather than a right*. When Bodin was trying to talk about our citizens and our townsmen, he blundered badly by confusing these two classes with one another. M. d'Alembert avoided that error in his article on Geneva, clearly distinguishing the four orders of men (or even five, counting mere foreigners) who dwell in our town, of which only two make up the republic. I don't know of any other French writer who has understood the real meaning of the word 'citizen'.

7. THE SOVEREIGN

This formula shows us that •the act of association involves a two-way commitment between the public and the individuals ·belonging to it·, and •that each individual, in making a con- tract with himself (so to speak), acquires two commitments: **(a)** as a member of the state he has a commitment to the sovereign, and **(b)** as a member of the sovereign [see Glossary] he has a commitment to each of the individuals, he being one of them. There is a maxim of civil law that no-one is bound by undertakings he has made to himself, but that doesn't apply here, because the present topic is incurring an obligation to •a whole of which

one is a part, and that is very different from incurring an obligation to
•oneself.

The proceeding I have been describing can't give the sovereign a commitment to itself. As I have just pointed out, an individual subject can
have a commitment to himself in this sense: as an individual he has a
commitment to the sovereign, and as a member of the sovereign he has
a commitment to himself. But the sovereign can't have a commitment
to itself; it doesn't have two distinct roles ·such that a commitment
could go from it in one role and towards it in the other·. For the sovereign to have a commitment to itself would be like an individual person
having a commitment to himself; it just isn't possible. And so it is
against the nature of the body politic for the sovereign to impose on
itself a law that it can't infringe: there isn't and can't be any kind of
basic law that is binding on the body of the people—even the social
contract itself can't do that. This doesn't mean that the body politic can't
enter into commitments with others [i.e. with other states]. .... It *can* do that,
because in relation to what is external to it—·i.e. in relation to other
states or sovereigns·—the sovereign is just a simple being, an individual.

But the body politic, i.e. the sovereign, owes its very existence to the
sanctity of *the contract*; so it can never commit itself, even to another
state, to do anything that conflicts with that original act e.g. to alienate
any part of itself, or to submit to another sovereign. ·I'm saying not that
the sovereign *ought* not to do such a thing, but that it *can't* do so·: violation of the act ·of contract-making· by which it exists would be self-

annihilation; and nothing can be created by something that has gone out of existence!

As soon as this multitude is united into one body in this way, any offence against one of the members is an attack on the body, and any offence against the body will be resented by the members. Thus, the two contracting parties—the individual member and the body politic—are obliged by duty and by self-interest to give each other help. . . .

Now, because the sovereign is made out of nothing but its constituent individuals, it doesn't and can't have any interest contrary to theirs; so there's no need for it to provide its subjects with guarantee ·of treating them well·, because •the body can't possibly wish to hurt all its members, and, as we'll see later on, *it can't hurt any individual one of them either.* The sovereign, merely by virtue of what it *is*, is always what it *ought to* be.

But the situation is different with respect to the relation of the subjects to the sovereign: despite their common interest, the sovereign would have no security that the subjects would behave as they have committed themselves to behaving unless it found some way to be assured of their fidelity.

The fact is that each individual •as a man can have a particular will that doesn't fit, and even conflicts with, the general will that he has *as a citizen.* His individual self-interest may speak to him quite differently from how the common interest does. He looks at the situation in this way:

"I have an absolute and naturally independent existence; I'm not something that exists only because certain items have come together in an association. So what I am said to *owe* to the common cause, i.e. to the body politic or sovereign whose existence *is* in that way dependent on the conduct of its members, is really a gift, a hand-out; if I withhold it, that won't harm anyone else as much as it will benefit me. As for the *moral person* that constitutes the state, that's not a man but a mere mental construct."

So he may wish to enjoy the rights of citizenship without being ready to fulfill the duties of a subject; and if that went on for long enough it would destroy the body politic.

To protect the social compact from being a mere empty formula, therefore, it silently includes the undertaking that anyone who refuses to obey the general will is to be compelled to do so by the whole body. This single item in the compact can give power to all the other items. It means nothing less than that each individual **will be forced to be free**. ·It's obvious how *forcing* comes into this, but. . . *to be free*? Yes·, because this is the condition which, by **giving** each citizen to his country, secures him against all personal dependence, ·i.e. secures him against being **taken** by anyone or anything else·. This is the key to the working of the political machine; it alone legitimises civil commitments which would otherwise be absurd, tyrannical, and liable to frightful abuses.

8. THE CIVIL STATE

This passage from •the state of nature to •the civil state produces a very remarkable change in man: the role that instinct used to play in his conduct is now taken over by ·a sense of· justice, and his actions now have a moral aspect that they formerly lacked. The voice of duty has taken over from physical impulses and ·a sense of what is *right has taken over from appetite*; and now—only now, the man who has until now considered only himself finds himself forced to act on different principles and to consult his reason before listening to his inclinations. In this *civil* state he is deprived of many advantages that he got from nature, but he gets enormous benefits in return—his faculties are so stimulated and developed, his ideas are extended, his feelings ennobled, and his whole soul uplifted. All this happens to such an extent that if the abuses of this new condition didn't often pull him down to something lower than he was in •the state of nature, he would be bound to bless continually the happy moment that took him from *it for ever*, and out of a dull and limited animal made a thinking being, a man.

Let us get a statement of profit and loss in terms that make it easy to compare the two sides. What man loses by the social contract is; his natural liberty and

- an unrestricted right to anything he wants and can get. What he gains
- civil liberty and
- the ownership of everything he possesses.

If we're to weigh these up accurately, we must distinguish

•**natural** liberty, which is limited only by the individual's powers, from

•**civil** liberty, which is limited by the general will. And we must distinguish

•**possession**, which is merely the effect of force or the principle of 'first come, first served', from

•**property**, which can only be based on a positive title. We could add on the 'profit' side the fact that in the civil state a man acquires moral liberty, which alone makes him truly

master of himself; for the drive of sheer appetite is •slavery, while obedience to a law that we prescribe to ourselves is •liberty. But I have said too much about this in other places; and the philosophical meaning of the word 'liberty' doesn't concern us here.

9. REAL ESTATE

At the moment when the community comes into existence, each of its members *gives himself to it*, himself just as he is, with any powers that he has, including all his possessions. It is *not* the case that this transfer of all his goods changes them from being •possessions in his hands to being •property in the hands of the sovereign; but because the city's powers are incomparably greater than any individual's, public pos- session is stronger and more irrevocable, without being any more legitimate. [The rest of this paragraph is expanded in ways that the ˙small dots˙ convention can't easily signify.] Actually, from the point of view of the members of this state its possession of each member's goods *[is* legitimate, because the state is the master of all their goods by the social contract which is the basis of all rights *within the state*. But that doesn't hold for foreigners,

225

because for them ownership depends solely on the 'first come, first served' principle, which also serves for states in their ownership of territory.

Of the two ways of getting a right to something in the state of nature, namely

being the first occupier of it, and

being the strongest,

(i) provides a right—'·first come, first served·'—that is more real than (ii) does; but it doesn't become a true right until *property*-rights are established. Every man has naturally a right to everything he needs; but the positive act that makes something his *property* excludes him from everything else.

Having acquired share, he ought to limit himself to that, and can't have any further claim on the community. That's why the first-occupier right, which is so weak in the state of nature, claims the respect of every man in civil society. What a man respects in this right is not so much •what belongs to someone else as •what doesn't belong to him.

In general, to authorize a first occupier's right over any bit of ground three conditions must be satisfied:

•the ground wasn't already occupied by someone else; •he occupies only as much as he needs for his subsistence;

•he takes possession of this ground not by an empty ceremony but by labour and cultivation.

His work on the land is the only sign of ownership that others should respect if he doesn't have a legal title.

In allowing the right of first occupancy on condition that the land was needed and was worked on, aren't we stretching that right as far as it can go? Could such a right be left with no limits or restrictions? To claim to be the master of a plot of common ground will it be enough merely to set foot on it? If a man has the strength to expel others for a moment, does that deprive them of any right to return? If a man or a people seize an immense territory and shut out the rest of the world, won't this be merely a *grab* that ought to be punished? ·The answer is surely 'yes'·, because such an act steals from others the living-space and means of subsistence that nature gave them in common. When Balboa stood on the sea-shore and took possession of the south seas and the whole of South America in the name of the Spanish crown, was that enough to dispossess all their actual inhabitants and to shut out from those territories all the princes of the world? If so, there's no need for all these ceremonies; the Catholic King can take possession of the whole universe all at once, tacking on a rider excluding from his claim any territories that were already possessed by other princes! We can imagine •how adjacent pieces of land belonging to individuals become, when they are combined, public territory, and •how the right of sovereignty over the sub- jects comes to be extended to being a right over their real estate. This makes the land-owners even more dependent ·on the sover- eign·; ·they have more to lose if things go wrong between them and the sovereign; and· this is a guarantee of their fidelity. The advantage of this apparently wasn't felt by ancient monarchs, who called themselves kings of **the Persians, the Scythians,** or **the Macedonians**, apparently regarding themselves as rulers of men rather than as masters of a country. Today's kings are cleverer: they call themselves kings of **France**, of **Spain**, of **England** and so on. Holding the land in this way, they are quite confident of holding the inhabitants.

This alienation in which individuals transfer their goods to the community has a special feature, namely that far from •depriving the individuals of their goods it •assures them of legitimate possession, changing; "I have taken possession of this (somehow)" into "I have a genuine right to this", and "I have the enjoyment of this" into "I own this".

Thus the possessors, •in their role as those to whom the public good has been entrusted, and, having their rights respected by all the state's members and maintained against foreign aggression by all its forces, have made a transfer that benefits both the public and still more themselves, thereby acquiring (as it were) everything that they gave up. This paradox is easily explained by distinguishing the sovereign's right from the owner's rights over the same estate—as we shall see later on.

It can also happen that men, begin to unite before they possess anything, subsequently occupy a tract of land that is enough for them all, and then, enjoy it in common, or share it out among themselves (either equally or in proportions fixed by the sovereign). But however the acquisition is made, each individual's right to his own estate is always subordinate to the community's right over everyone's estate; without this, the social tie would be fragile and the exercise of sovereignty would be feeble.

To bring this chapter and this book to an end, I'll remark on a fact that should be the basis for any social system, namely: The basic compact doesn't **destroy** natural inequality; rather, it **replaces** •such physical inequalities as nature may have set up between men by •an equality that is moral and legitimate, so that men who may be unequal in strength or intelligence become equal by agreement and legal right.

Under bad governments, this equality is only apparent and illusory: all it does is to keep the pauper in his poverty and the rich man in the position he has usurped. Laws in fact are always useful to those who have possessions and harmful to those who don't; from which it follows that the social state is advantageous to men only when everyone has something and no-one has too much.

PART 1 OF BOOK 2

1. SOVEREIGNTY IS INALIENABLE

The first and most important consequence of the principles I have laid down is that the directing of the state in the light of the object for which it was instituted, i.e. the common good, must be done by the general will. The •clashing of particular interests made it •necessary to establish a society, and the •agreement of those same interests made it •possible to do so. It's the common element in these different interests that forms the social tie; and if there were there nothing that they all had in common, no society could exist. It is solely by this common interest that every society should be governed.

I hold then that sovereignty, being nothing less than the exercise of the general will, can never be alienated [see Glossary], and that the sovereign, which is nothing but a collective being, can't be represented except by itself: the power indeed may be transmitted, but not the will.

Perhaps a particular will *could* agree on some point with the general will, but at least it's impossible for such an agreement to be lasting and constant. Why? Because it's of the very nature of a particular will to tend towards •favouritism, be •partial [i.e. to favour some people over others], whereas the general will tends towards •equality. It is even more impossible to have any guarantee of this agreement; for even if it did always exist that would be the effect not of skill but of chance. The sovereign may indeed say:
'Right now I will what that man wills (or at least what
he says he wills)', but it can't say because it's absurd for the will to bind itself for the future, and no will is obliged to consent to anything that isn't for the good of the being whose will it is. If then the populace promises simply to *obey*, by that very act it dissolves itself and loses what makes it *a people*; the moment a master exists, there is no longer a sovereign, and from that moment the body politic has ceased to exist.

This isn't to deny that rulers' commands can count as general wills, if the sovereign is free to oppose them and doesn't do so. In such a case, universal silence should be taken to show the people's consent. I'll explain this fully later on.

2. SOVEREIGNTY IS INDIVISIBLE

For the same reason that makes it inalienable, sovereignty is indivisible. Here is why. Either will **(a)** is general[4] or it **(b)** isn't; it is the will either of **(a)** the body of the people or of **(b)** only a part of it. When it is declared, then, either **(a)** it is an act of sovereignty and constitutes law, or **(b)** it is merely a particular will or

the rest of the sentence: *un acte de magistrature ; c'est un décret tout au plus.*

which literally means: an act of magistracy—at the most a decree.

what Rousseau was getting at: regulations laid down by high-level bureaucrats, not basic laws issuing from the legislature, the sovereign. [Re 'magistracy', see Glossary.]

'What that man wills tomorrow, I too shall will',

To be general, a will need not always be unanimous; but every vote must be counted: any exclusion is a breach of generality.

But our political theorists, unable to divide sovereignty on the basis of its •source, divide it according to its •object. They divide it into:

•force and will,

•legislative power and executive power, •rights of taxation, justice and war, •internal affairs and foreign relations.

Sometimes they run these sections together and sometimes they separate them; they turn the sovereign into a fantastic being composed of several connected pieces: it is as if they were making man of several bodies, one with eyes, one with arms, another with feet, and each with nothing else! We're told that the jugglers of Japan dismember a child before the eyes of the spectators; then they throw the pieces into the air one after another, and the child falls down alive and whole. The conjuring tricks of our political theorists are pretty much like that: having dismembered the body politic by a huckster's trick they then reassemble it. . . somehow!

This error comes from a failure to think precisely about the sovereign authority, regarding as different •parts of it what are really just different •emanations from it.

[Rousseau seems to mean that they are just different actions that are per- formed under the authority of the sovereign. In distinguishing (a) parts of the sovereign authority from (b) actions performed not by the sovereign authority but by subordinate governmental agencies, he may be distinguishing parts of x from actions of x, or distinguishing the sovereign's actions from those of subordinate agencies.

In fact he seems to be thinking only of the second of these distinctions. Read on.]

Thus, for example, the acts of declaring war and making peace have been regarded as acts of sovereignty, but they aren't. None of them are laws; each of them simply applies a law to a particular case, involving a decision ·not about what the law is to be, but only· about how the law applies in this case. This will be clear when the idea attached to the word 'law' has been fixed.

If we track the other divisions in the same way, we would find that whenever anyone takes sovereignty to be divided there is a mistake: the rights that are taken as being part of sovereignty are really all subordinate, and always presuppose the existence of supreme wills that they are merely applying.

This lack of exactness has thrown a cloud of obscurity over the conclusions of writers on political right who have laid down principles on the basis of which to pass judgment on the respective rights of kings and peoples. When I try to say how much obscurity, words fail me! Everyone can see in Grotius's work (Book 1 chapters 3 and 4) how the learned man and his translator, Barbeyrac, entangle and confuse themselves with in their own sophistries, for fear of saying too little or too much of what they think, and so offending the interests they have to placate. Grotius, a refugee in France, discontented with his own country [Holland], and wanting to pay court to Louis XIII, to whom his book is dedicated, will go to any lengths to strip the peoples of all their rights and clothe kings in them with every conceivable decoration. This would also have been much to the taste of Barbeyrac, who dedicated his translation to George I of England. But unfortunately ·for him· the expulsion of James II, which Barbeyrac called his 'abdication', compelled him to be on his guard, to shuffle and switch positions, in order to avoid making William ·of Orange, who succeeded James on the throne· a usurper. If these two writers had adopted the true principles, all ·their· difficulties would have been removed, and they would have been always consistent; but they'd have told the truth *sadly*, and they wouldn't have been paying court to anyone except the people. Well, the truth is no road to fortune, and the populace doesn't give out ambassadorships, university chairs, or pensions.

CONCLUSION

Now that I have laid down the true principles of political right, and tried to plant the state on its own base, the next task would be to strengthen it by its foreign relations. That would bring in the law of nations, commerce, the right of war and conquest, public law, leagues, negotiations, treaties, etc. But all this adds up to a new subject that is far too vast for my narrow scope. As it is, I have ranged further afield than I ought to have.

11: TWO TREATISES OF GOVERNMENT

In the Former, The False Principles and Foundation of Sir Robert Filmer, and His Followers, Are Detected and Overthrown: The Latter, Is an Essay Concerning the Original, Extent, and End, of Civil Government.
John Locke

The complete text of these two treatises can be accessed using the following links. They are over 250 pages and as such it would be wasteful to reproduce the complete Treatises in this volume. The copy and translation available via the links is in the public domain and you may read it at your will and leisure.

Download the full pdf
https://bit.ly/john_locke

TTI: FUNERAL BLUES

By W.H.Audun[63] (published 1936)

Stop all the clocks, cut off the telephone,
Prevent the dog from barking with a juicy bone,
Silence the pianos and with muffled drum
Bring out the coffin, let the mourners come.

Let aeroplanes circle moaning overhead
Scribbling on the sky the message 'He is Dead'.
Put crepe bows round the white necks of the public doves,
Let the traffic policemen wear black cotton gloves.

He was my North, my South, my East and West,
My working week and my Sunday rest,
My noon, my midnight, my talk, my song;
I thought that love would last forever: I was wrong.

The stars are not wanted now; put out every one,
Pack up the moon and dismantle the sun,
Pour away the ocean and sweep up the wood;
For nothing now can ever come to any good.

_____

---

[63] *Wystan Hugh Auden (21 February 1907 – 29 September 1973), who published as W. H. Auden, was an Anglo-American poet, born in England, later an American citizen, regarded by many critics as one of the greatest writers of the 20th century. His work is noted for its stylistic and technical achievements, its engagement with moral and political issues, and its variety of tone, form and content. The central themes of his poetry are love, politics and citizenship, religion and morals, and the relationship between unique human beings and the anonymous, impersonal world of nature.*

Printed in Great Britain
by Amazon